PRAISE FOR PRACTICAL CONSCIOUS CREATION

"*Practical Conscious Creation* is an extraordinary gateway to anchoring manifesting and law of attraction into your daily activities to create a life of YOUR choosing, vision, ease and prosperity. A life-changing book!"

> **MARIE DIAMOND**, transformational leader and speaker and star of *The Secret*

"Law of Attraction Blah-blah-blah, it's a lovely idea, but ideas without a practical application have left large groups of disillusioned people in their wake. Finally someone steps up and gives you the nuts and bolts of *Practical Conscious Creation*. This book breaks it down, showing you how to take Conscious Creation from a general concept into everyday practice. If you are fed up with the empty promises from the Law of Attraction crowd, get your knife and fork out and dig into this meaty material."

> **DOV BARON**, Elite Mind Strategist, Best Selling Author, creator of the CORE Affluence System for Leadership, and Host of *The Accidental Guru Show*

"I consider myself an attraction connoisseur, and a snobby one at that! I love someone who can speak to the practical ways to integrate how to be a conscious creator. I've always loved Jackie's way of teaching these principles because she is right on target and always consistent in her message. There are very few people who I'll even pay attention to on this topic, but Jackie is one of them!"

> **JEANNA GABELLINI**, co-author of *Life Lessons on Mastering the Law of Attraction*

"It's not always easy to remember to be a Conscious Creator or to practice the principles of law of attraction and positive energy. And that's why *Practical Conscious Creation* is so powerful! It helps you anchor those principles into a way of life—into everything you do!"

> **CHRISTINE KLOSER**, author of *The Freedom Formula*

"As humanity awakens into oneness, it is vitally important to be conscious of our own thought patterns. With optimism and sincerity, Jackie Lapin encourages us to examine our personal frequency and raise our vibration to the highest level possible. This book will teach you to broadcast energy that will improve your relationships, workplace, and personal life so you c   rerse."

> **CHARLENE**   *ss Gospel:*
> *Birthing the (*

PRAISE FOR PRACTICAL CONSCIOUS CREATION

"Jackie Lapin has done it! *Practical Conscious Creation* provides a concise road map for implementing daily innovative, creative imagery and inspired actions in ways that result in both incremental and life-changing alterations. If you are looking to have more health, wealth and overall prosperity, this book will take you there."

> KEN D. FOSTER, bestselling author *Ask and You Will Succeed*

"I like this book! It points in the direction mankind is clearly headed: an age of solution-consciousness rather than of problem-consciousness. As my guru Paramhansa Yogananda put it, 'The greater the will power, the greater the flow of energy.' *Practical Conscious Creation* is about clearing away the cobwebs that prevent people from thinking greatness!"

> SWAMI KRIYANANDA, worldwide spiritual leader, author of 140 books including the award winning *The New Path: My Life with Paramhansa Yogananda* and last living, still-teaching disciple of Yogananda.

"*Practical Conscious Creation* makes conscious manifesting a way of life! Here's the key to applying it everywhere, in every circumstance so that you can create a life of ease, success and prosperity."

> PEGGY MCCOLL, New York Times best-selling author of *Your Destiny Switch*

green press INITIATIVE

Findhorn Press is committed to preserving ancient forests and natural resources. We elected to print this title on 30% post consumer recycled paper, processed chlorine free. As a result, for this printing, we have saved:

13 Trees (40' tall and 6-8" diameter)
5 Million BTUs of Total Energy
1,316 Pounds of Greenhouse Gases
5,936 Gallons of Wastewater
376 Pounds of Solid Waste

Findhorn Press made this paper choice because our printer, Thomson-Shore, Inc., is a member of Green Press Initiative, a nonprofit program dedicated to supporting authors, publishers, and suppliers in their efforts to reduce their use of fiber obtained from endangered forests.

For more information, visit www.greenpressinitiative.org

Environmental impact estimates were made using the Environmental Defense Paper Calculator. For more information visit: www.papercalculator.org.

FSC
www.fsc.org
MIX
Paper from responsible sources
FSC® C013483

Practical Conscious Creation

Daily Techniques to Manifest Your Desires

Jackie Lapin

FINDHORN PRESS

First published by Findhorn Press 2011

ISBN 978-1-84409-561-2

British Library Cataloguing-in-Publication Data.
A catalogue record for this book is available from the British Library.

Edited by Nicky Leach
Cover design and illustrations by Richard Crookes
Layout by Thierry Bogliolo
Printed and bound in the USA

1 2 3 4 5 6 7 8 9 10 16 15 14 13 12 13 12 11

Published by
Findhorn Press
117-121 High Street
Forres IV36 1AB
Scotland, UK

t +44(0)1309 690582
f +44(0)131 777 2711
e info@findhornpress.com
www.findhornpress.com

Contents

Introduction

Wouldn't life be better if your every act and thought contributed to creating a happy, healthy, prosperous, and rewarding existence?

You can indeed become the architect of your dream life by seizing the opportunity to incorporate Practical Conscious Creation into every aspect of your existence—essentially learning a new way to live—a way to harness universal energy, so that you are flowing with the positive momentum that makes life easy and opens the doors of opportunity and abundance.

Using the guidance in this book you will be inspired to transform each day into a gateway to your new life. On every page, you will find creative and dynamic processes that are the building blocks for your future. These easy-to-implement and fun techniques make learning to be a Conscious Creator second nature.

But first let's explore what Conscious Creation is and why practicing it daily will alter your life is the most miraculous ways.

Conscious Creation is the act of choosing the future you want to experience and then setting in motion the vibrational energy to create or attract it. Conscious Creation is much more than the law of attraction, a universal law popularized by the hugely popular DVD and book *The Secret*. Many people have unsuccessfully tried to manifest using visualization techniques proposed by *The Secret* and failed because they don't see or understand the larger process at work.

As I revealed in my earlier best-selling book, *The Art of Conscious Creation: How You Can Transform the World,* Conscious Creation is a process of what I call "Personal Energy Management," coupled with specific mental and emotional energy projections and practices. Without learning Personal Energy Management, the process of positive, conscious manifestation is doomed to fail.

Here's how and why Personal Energy Management works:

The entire Universe—what we see and what we don't—consists of a huge interconnecting web of energy. We are beings of vibrating energy, and since our thoughts and emotions are simply extensions of us—waves of frequency— they interact with the rest of the world, impacting in either a positive or negative way. Our energetic emissions create a domino or a giant daisy chain effect. Thus, the energy we emit goes forth and changes the fabric of the future. Quantum physics is showing how conscious thought can and does impact the world. Thanks to the work of some extraordinary researchers, there is a growing body of illuminating studies that demonstrate *what we think, we create!*

Now, our thoughts and emotions are either vibrating in the high range of the frequency scale or the low range. The high (positive) range includes thoughts and feelings such as love, joy, compassion, gratitude, kindness, acceptance, trust in the universe, self-love, and so on. The low (negative) frequencies include fear, anger, distrust, jealousy, self-contempt or disregard, dissatisfaction, blame, victimization, guilt, and so on.

The Universe vibrates at the highest level—LOVE. If you are vibrating in the high range of the frequency scale, you are vibrating with the Universe; you are sharing the same wavelength. It is what I call "surfing the love vibration." This is like drafting in a racecar or having the wind in your sails. Life is going to be easier and effortless, much more free of struggle. Synchronicities occur that bring people and resources to you. And most significantly, you are manifesting what you consciously desire faster and faster!

Now here's what happens if you are vibrating in the low range: it is like driving a car with the brakes on. Life isn't much fun. You're constantly hitting resistance and having to take detours. Things just never seem to work out the way you want. Your relationship is falling apart. You're unhappy at your job. You're not making enough money. You feel like a victim. All of these things are happening because your vibration is going against the Universe's.

Have you met anyone who's constantly complaining that the world is out to get them? If so, then you know someone living in the low-frequency range who is attracting back exactly what they are emitting and expecting. If you are vibrating on a low frequency, you attract unwelcome, unhappy, destructive experiences.

So the key to Conscious Creation is taking responsibility for and managing your personal frequency—your energy emissions. This means choosing the thoughts and emotions you want to have—and eliminating or dissipating those that are harmful to you and only lend themselves to the unconscious creation that attracts unpleasant and dissatisfying experiences. Happy, loving, gracious thoughts and emotions create a happy life.

Managing your personal frequency is Job One when you are a Conscious Creator. Once you've swept your energy field clean of negative vibrations, then the next step is to fix your sights on what it is exactly you want to experience, so the Universe can get a clear message and deliver it. If there is no clarity, it can't fill your order. The following sequence in the process is to create the images of what you wish to experience and then project them. This is just like projecting a movie on a screen. But in this case, the screen consists of the particles of energy that will form into your desired reality through the intention you have issued.

Setting large life intentions is a powerful means of moving toward Consciously Creating your dream existence, but the Universe is most responsive to your daily efforts to live at a higher frequency, positively visualize your life and solve problems. You'll find that not only are your dreams coming closer to reality or are already manifesting but each day is more joyful, peaceful, and satisfying.

The chapters and individual sections in this book are carefully organized to show you ways to adapt this new life philosophy to all that you do—from banishing fearful feelings and thoughts (see the section "Fear: The Siren Call to Change") to dealing with problem in-laws at the holidays (See the section "Don't Let Your Relatives Ring Your Holiday Bell"); from making difficult decisions (see the section "What Would My Soul Do?") to minding and growing your resources (see the section "A Dialogue Between You and Your Money"); from dealing with challenging relationships (see the section "How to Stay Positive with a Negative Energy Spouse") to business success (see the section "Conscious Creation in the Workplace").

Each of the 70 Practical Conscious Creation Tips sprinkled throughout this book features specific actions or steps that you can take to raise your frequency, create positive visualizations, and keep focused on the energy habits that will make you a Master Manifestor. You'll find that many of them are fun!

These tips are merely a starting point. Once you have absorbed the information in them and started to put it into practice, you can add to your collection of tips by logging on to **www.practicalconsciouscreation.com/vault** twice a month to read new ones. In this way, you will have an ever-expanding toolbox of ideas to keep you pointed in the Conscious Creation direction.

May you Consciously Create all you desire!

Practical Conscious Creation Tip No. 1

Life is a Journey, Not a Destination

Just when I needed it, this wonderful piece of wisdom showed up in my life, and it now has a beautiful spot above the mantle in my house. It's a reminder not to defer all sense of joy to the future, thinking that life is still ahead. That "if I get everything done, then I can play." Play all along the way. Enjoy every brilliant day. Love whomever you are with. Savor each moment of work, play, and quiet introspection. Don't be so hard on yourself. Look for the wonder in all things. Take the time to pamper yourself. The journey is just as enriching as the destination. Living life this way will open the door for better, faster manifesting!

Chapter 1

Honing Your Conscious Creation Skills

The world is divided into two types of people: Conscious Creators and Unconscious Creators. Most people fall into the latter category. They don't understand why their life is falling apart, why their job makes them unhappy, and why they can't attract the right partner. They feel victimized, angry, or depressed. Unconscious creators are manifesting most of their own misery unconsciously!

Conscious creators, on the other hand, have a clear vision about what they want to have happen, respect that their future is within their own hands, have the ultimate trust that everything will turn out alright, and continue to put out kind, loving, positive energy—regardless of what happens to them. Furthermore, they have the power to contribute to manifesting a better world for everyone!

Are You A Conscious Creator? Do You Have What It Takes to Make Your Dreams Come True?

The thing that determines the difference between the two is how you use your energy! This means that if you put out negative energy, you will attract more of it. If you put out positive, loving energy, you will draw back more positive experiences.

Positive and Negative Energy Habits

Unconscious Creators have "negative energy habits." They dwell on the past and worry about the future. They have control issues and don't trust the future to anyone but themselves. They may have self-esteem problems, anger directed internally or at others, and display an inability to appropriately communicate their emotions in a positive manner. They blame others, dwell on everything that's wrong, and listen to all kinds of irritating voices in their minds that point out their failings. They live in fear that they are unworthy and someone will find out, or that they won't get their share of the world's pie. They are curt with others, in a hurry to get to the head of the line, have to win, wish to have more than everyone else, want attention now! They assume something or someone is out to get the better of them. They don't trust others, they blame everyone else, they are sure the Universe "has it in for them," or they hang their head in shame because it must be their fault that everything is wrong. They seldom slow down and listen to their heart. They are entirely in their head and their egos. They allow all this negative energy to pave their future path, and they don't realize the damage they are inflicting on themselves and the world.

Conscious Creators, on the other hand, have "positive energy habits." These are the world's optimists. They envision something they want or desire to have happen, and they take positive steps in that direction. They trust the Universe to bring to them what is in their highest good. They always look on the bright side of any problems they encounter. They are kind and loving, thoughtful and straightforward with all those they meet and the people they care about. They deal with their frustrations in a positive, communicative way, and they let go. They don't dwell on things, since they have released their roadblocks. They continue to move forward instead of being mired in the past. They are far more likely to be living and enjoying the present moment than bartering it for the future. They don't blame others, but try to be compassionate with people who delay them from accomplishing their goals, and they figure out their role in a situation when things don't go smoothly. They understand the value of forgiveness. They don't project their fears on other people; instead, they assume that others will help them succeed. They listen to their heart and act on the goodness within their soul. And they maintain a healthy, sustained dialogue with the Universe. They allow their positive energy to open amazing doors for them!

Can Someone Choose to Become a Conscious Creator?

Absolutely! The key is to consciously begin changing your thinking. You can choose to have positive thoughts and banish the negative ones. You can choose to handle a situation with a cool head instead of a hot head. You can choose to be more loving, kind, and compassionate. You can choose to attract abundance, instead of repelling it. You can begin to envision the kind of life you want to live and become that life.

What Can You Do If You Become a Conscious Creator?

You can transform your life—create incredible loving relationships and friendships, change the way you look, improve your health, get a better job or gain more respect at the office, follow your heart to create a new business or type of job that's just right for you, manifest more time for leisure, have a greater appreciation for the abundance that surrounds you, develop more personal freedom, improve your home life, attract greater wealth, or feel loved. It's all just a choice away!

Practical Conscious Creation Tip No. 2

Your Words as Harbingers

Since our words are energy emissions that impact our future, it behooves us to watch carefully what we say and how we say it. It is vital we reframe our words to reflect what we want to experience, rather than what we fear we will experience. That is why you will always want to refer to "opportunities" instead of "problems" and change insecurity to surety (I'll try versus I will). Be cognizant of when you are projecting your doubts, fears, and limitations with your words, and change these to demonstrate your optimism and faith. The future that you paint with words is the future that you will experience. So choose your words wisely, and you will create stepping stones for a life well lived.

Switching Thoughts and Changing Gears

If you want to join the ranks of the Conscious Creators, visualizing and manifesting a more satisfying life, you'll have to leave your negative energy habits behind. Here are a few ways to do that:

Switch your thoughts. Monitor your thoughts. If you are thinking something negative, just flip it over to something more positive. From "I'm disappointed my vacation is cancelled" to "Now I can tour all of those museums near my home that I wanted to see." From "My girlfriend dumped me" to "I learned a great deal in this relationship and look forward to applying it positively in the next one." Don't dwell, don't rehash, don't fixate, don't blame, don't fume, don't judge, don't feel like a victim. Instead, feel powerful and act with positive intent. Think about how you can become a better, more compassionate person toward yourself and others. Be the positive, upbeat person you like to be around—the one the world just seems to bless. You start that process in your head.

Change your focus. Stop asking "What is wrong with my life?" and start asking "What is right with my life?"

Change your words. Let your mind be the gatekeeper of your tongue. Think before you speak. Instead of saying words that subtly imply your own limitations and failures—or someone else's—change the words you use. Put them in a positive framework. Speak with limitless possibility and faith in the future. Refrain from gossiping or complaining. Speak to people with consideration and use your words to make a positive bridge, even when there is disagreement. Make the words that come out of your mouth footsteps to a great future.

Go for a walk. Speaking of footsteps. . . When you feel a funk coming on, or when you are angry, get up and go for a walk. Use the time not to dwell on grievances but to undertake an attitude adjustment. Look at the trees, listen to the birds, love the sun. Think about how good life is and how you can make it better. Feel the emotion when relaxing. Allow the goodwill to wash over you. If music makes you feel more upbeat, then walk with your iPod tuned to your favorite songs.

Be in the moment—love the moment. To get out of the negative rehashing of the past or fixation of the future, do something novel—be in the moment.

Breathe deeply, listen to what's going on around you, go sniff a flower, cuddle the dog. Just enjoy that very moment and love it for its presence.

Imagine your joy. So maybe it hasn't been a great day. If that's the case, just imagine your joy. Put your feet up and remember some fantastic moment of your life. Or create a vision of the future that brings you joy. Let yourself revel in that experience. The emotion of joy attracts more joy.

Do a random act of kindness. If you really want to feel good about life, help someone else. It may be someone you know and love or somebody you have never met before. Just do something nice, and it will raise your positive energy. Do it more than once and you'll be forming a new positive energy habit!

Put yourself in someone else's shoes. Before you jump on someone for their "stupidity, mistakes, just-doing-my-job role," put yourself in their shoes. Maybe that person has a wife who's critically ill, hasn't had the benefit of your level of education, or came from a culture that has different values. Instead, come from a place of understanding and compassion, and your own stock will rise in goodwill and positive energy.

Give yourself the gift of being with high-energy people. Change the company you keep. Find people who are positive, upbeat, kind, thoughtful, and optimistic. Look for fellow Conscious Creators—they may teach you something!

Be true to yourself. If you are unhappy with your job, your co-workers, your relationship, or your status in the world, either leave and find a new path or change the situation using positive energy, thoughts, deeds, and diplomacy. But most of all, be true to yourself. Don't stay in a miserable situation because you are "stuck." Be honest with yourself about what is working and not working.

Give yourself a break. Don't be too hard on yourself. Negative energy is not always directed at others. Forgive yourself; recognize that it's okay to be "imperfect" and that you are really an incredible human being! Ask all your friends what they love about you.

Have an attitude of gratitude. Count your blessings every day. Say thanks to the Universe for all the good things in your life. Remind yourself how fortunate you really are.

Practical Conscious Creation Tip No. 3

Sweet Dreams

Turn off *The Tonight Show*! Tune out the news! Close up the laptop and stop chatting with your Facebook "friends." When you go to bed tonight, you have a new assignment. Set an intention! Or even a few intentions. Let the Universe work on your wish while you are getting your beauty sleep. There is power in setting an intention at night. It works on your subconscious and helps create shifts in consciousness and awareness. As you slip into alpha brain wave state, setting an intention for the night makes it easier for your wavelengths to get in sync with the Universe. That will speed up your manifesting ability. So state your wishes for yourself personally (how you'd like to change) and for what you desire to come forth. Sweet, sweet dreams!

Spout love! Whenever in doubt, spout love! Love, kindness, and compassion are the emotions and thoughts that resonate most powerfully with the Universe. These will not only come back to you but they will help you pave a pathway to your new reality.

Do these things and you will clear the path to becoming a Conscious Creator, manifesting the future you desire!

Consciously Creating Your Day

Most of us go about our lives each day feeling like wind chimes—sometimes we make lovely sweet music and sometimes we are buffeted by gale force winds, with wild dissonant sounds. Often we feel at the mercy of fate, which is handing us some good days and some days that are filled with roadblocks, obstacles, annoyances, and frustrations. At the end of the day we're so tired from dealing with challenges we just collapse in a heap, with little energy left over to enjoy our families, friends, or quiet time at home.

But what if we could actually shape our day before it begins? How would life be if we could order our day, just like we order breakfast? Can I have some fast-and-easy approval on my report, along with my coffee today, Miss? I'll take some pancakes with my on-time air flight!

"Dream on," you say? Well actually, yes, that's exactly what you can do to make almost every day a "dream day." You must imagine your next 24 hours in advance. It's called Consciously Creating Your Day.

Conscious Creation is the act of aligning yourself with the Universe and setting intentions

So on any given day, if your thoughts are negative—perhaps you've had a fight with your husband or you feel guilty for eating a pint of ice cream the night before—you will begin your day by attracting all kinds of other unpleasant consequences. It may start in the morning when you accidentally spill the coffee on your skirt, continue when your computer malfunctions, and end when you run out of gas on the way home, even though the gauge says "full." Have you ever noticed how bad days escalate? Though you may not be aware of it, you are helping to manifest your own heartache and problems.

On the other hand, if you begin the day feeling joyful, happy to be alive, at one with the world, and excited about what you will do that day, it is likely that your day will continue to be a winner. And even if you are faced with an obstacle, you will handle it with aplomb and it will disappear quickly. You experience ease, speedy action on your desires, and effectiveness. You are drawing to yourself experiences that support your own sense of goodwill.

So can you actually control having more good days? Yes, you can! You can begin a practice of daily Conscious Creation.

Each day before you begin your workday or you embark on your tasks for the morning, you can do the following:

- Create a special sanctuary, somewhere you can feel comfortable. Turn off the cell phone and take the landline off the hook for a few minutes.

- Get quiet and put yourself into a meditative or quiet state. Close your eyes.

- Breathe deeply several times.

- Imagine a golden cord of light from your tailbone into the earth and another from the top of your head upward. Each of these cords is fed by a pool of beautiful golden energy that heals you, fuels you, and imbues you with joy.

- Allow the feeling of goodwill to flood into you. Just feel your alignment with the Universe, as love, ease, comfort, and happiness flow through every cell in your body.

- Now begin to create a vision for your day. What would you like to see happen? How would it unfold? Who would be there?

- Shoo away any thoughts of the problems that could arise or the argument that is building up with your boss. Instead see yourself spreading a net of compassion and care over him or her, working together collaboratively to resolve any outstanding issues.

- Envision great meetings, clients handing you a check, tasks getting accomplished easily and effortlessly, co-workers supporting you, a great work environment, supervisors offering you praise and a raise, your creativity flowing, your problem-solving skills at their peak, your team getting a big win, you being given a great assistant who can take some of the workload... See all activities being peaceful, successful, and conflict-free.

- Imagine everything happening at home just as you would like—support from your family for household chores, a loving environment, your spouse or partner showing his or her romantic side, peace and quiet so you can relax, everyone healthy, great nutritious food on the table, time for you to exercise or go to yoga, a playful walk with your dog, beautiful time with your children or your companions. . .

• Create magnificent mind pictures of the day you really want to experience— the perfect day! Feel like you are there! Experience all the fabulous emotions of that exceptional day. Let those happy, joyful, satisfying emotions help draw it to you!

• Say thanks to the Universe for *already* granting this dream day. Put forth your gratitude.

• Then let go! Give the outcome over to the Universe and trust that it is looking after your highest good.

• Slowly open your eyes and greet your day!

By Consciously Creating your day, you are increasing the odds that you will indeed have a felicitous experience. This is not to say that you won't encounter problems and obstacles, but you will have reduced the number and the degree, and more importantly, put yourself into a calm and productive mindset to deal with the situation in a positive and effective way, instead of escalating the problem with negative energy that you dispense unconsciously. Life will become more effortless, struggle-free, stress-free, and enjoyable. You'll have energy left over at the end of the day to play, entertain friends, share experiences with your husband, or interact with your children.

What is truly exciting about Conscious Creation is that it is so empowering. You have the ability to shape and mold your own future—one day at a time. What could be better than that?

Manifesting: What Has Gone Wrong When It Doesn't Work

Why is it that some people seem to be able to easily manifest their desires and others get frustrated and just give up? Why do some people seem to have the golden touch and others get disillusioned and think manifesting is a bunch of bunk?

That's because manifesting is like a car. Each part of the system has to be

Practical Conscious Creation Tip No. 4

Get Into the Flow

Here's a practice that will really start your day power-fully—consciously aligning with universal energy. Each morning before I start work, I stand before a big picture window and drink in the beauty outside. I spread my legs wide and center myself and bring my hands to my chest in a prayer position. I take a deep breath. I envision golden light bathing me from above. As I do, I press my hands together and lift them toward the sky. I recite to the Universe that "I am in the flow," and then allow my hands to part, facing outward/downward and circle back down to my outer thighs. I do this at least four times. I also then verbally invite the glorious energy of the day into my life. If I've had a negative day the previous day, I release all negative energy into the earth, then again wel-come the fresh energy. I can only tell you that on days that I forget to do this practice or am too busy to make the time, my days do not go as smoothly as when I make sure to consciously connect to the universal energy flow.

functioning effectively in order for the engine to work and the car to drive forward. If any portion is out of alignment or nonfunctional, then you won't be going anywhere. So let me provide a simple checklist to make sure all the parts are working!

Here are all the systems that need to be working properly for you to manifest optimally and rapidly:

1. **You've injected "high personal frequency."** Make sure you have filled your tank with high vibrations. This makes all the other parts work at peak performance. Operating with joy, hope, confidence, love, compassion, trust, and so on in your tank allows the manifesting to happen; low-vibration energy won't power the vehicle.

2. **Is this good for you?** Does it diminish or take advantage of others? Check the gauge. If it says that your highest good is the ultimate goal, and you're not hurting others, then you are good to go.

3. **You've turned the whine off.** If you are whining and complaining, sorry, go back to the garage. Your "manifesting engine" runs on pure positive thoughts and desires.

4. **Your windows are clear and you can see the direction you are going.** Clarity is essential. If your windows are fogged up, and if you are in any way confused about the direction, then you are destined to wander all over creation and back. Once you have clarity, your "manifesting vehicle" can take you where you want to go.

5. **The seats are comfortable and all the outside noise is eliminated.** If you're not really comfortable and you're getting all kinds of distractions, then your driving will be erratic. Your engine and your interior have to be in sync to make manifesting happen.

6. **The driver has to commit the time and focus.** Make sure that you can give yourself enough time to drive to your destination. You can't shortchange the process, and the focus must be consistent.

7. **The "imagination gear" is engaged.** Open this up to its fullest! Go for full speed and distance. Reach for the horizon; don't just settle for what's close. You'll be limiting yourself if you do. Let your visualizing gear be expansive. Remember to visualize your destination as if you were already there!

8. **Turn off the "how? switch."** You really don't need to know this to manifest; you just need to focus on your ultimate destination. Your automatic

Practical Conscious Creation Tip No. 5

Initiate Your Conscious Creation Log

Start your Conscious Creation log! Begin recording those desires that you are choosing to manifest. Jot each one down as you complete your visioning process, or as you simply think of them, including the date. Then check off each of the ones that come true, and also specify that date. You'll have a way of looking back to see how effectively and how quickly you are manifesting. The more success you have, the more excited you will be at the results and the more deliberate you will become in setting your future course.

Global Positioning System (GPS) will take care of how you are getting to your desired location.

9. **Trust the "manufacturer."** Don't question whether it's working. Don't try to maintain or wrestle control of your manifesting vehicle. If you do, your stubbornness may take you down a wrong path. Let the manifesting vehicle do what it's supposed to, since it has a very trusted manufacturer—proven over time.

10. **Disengage.** Once your manifesting vehicle is in motion, disengage. You don't have to drive the same route again and again. The vehicle knows what's in your itinerary and will take you there. Let go and you'll get there with ease and grace.

11. **Watch for signs.** Now you might see signs that are meant to guide you along to your destination. Be looking for them. Don't ignore them, because you ignore them at your peril. You'll miss the right turnoff, lose a key short-cut, or end up on a dirt road somewhere. This could compel you to start over.

12. **Be patient and grateful.** Give yourself plenty of time to reach your manifesting destination. Impatience can stall the vehicle. Remember it's not your timetable that will get you there; it's the manufacturer's. Patience and gratitude will be rewarded with a lovely, relaxing, and fun journey that ends in a remarkable destination of your choice.

Frequency Matching: The Power of Resonance

Much is written about the "law of attraction" and its ability to draw to you unpleasant experiences if you are vibrating on a negative wave length and unconsciously manifesting. But one powerful aspect of the law of attraction that is often forgotten is the specific formula for attracting what you do want: frequency matching.

At the very basis of this universal principle is one simple concept that makes living by the law of attraction easy to remember and practice. We know that energy attracts or repels. So the fastest and most effective way to bring something to you is to match the energy of that you want to attract. You must resonate what you wish to be or what you wish to attract. "Being leads to having and having leads to being."

For example, if you wish to become wealthy, you must project the energy of wealth and prosperity. If you want to attract love, you must project the energy of love, acceptance, and compassion. If you wish to experience companionship with supportive new friends, then be a supportive and caring friend.

In order to bring it to you—whatever it is—you must already be emitting that energy, in some tangible, thoughtful, or emotional way.

This doesn't mean that you must already be wealthy. It isn't just that the wealthy get wealthier, although that is certainly likely if they exude joy and gratitude over their prosperity. It's more about how you feel! If you are a person of little means, but you feel wealthy in spirit and love in whatever you do have, then you can attract greater means. Here are ways you can "frequency-match":

- Action: Perform actions that put you in the situation where you would experience what you are trying to attract. Dress up and dine in Beverly Hills. Fly first class on a short flight where you get pampered. Put on your best workout clothes and go work out where the well-to-do work out if you want to feel moneyed. If you intend to have more fun, do kids' things—fingerpaint, build sand castles, ride bicycles. Be what you want to become.

- Thinking/Imagination: Use your mental energy to create visions and scenarios where you are experiencing that which you want to attract. Imagine putting thousands of dollars into a bank account from a new investment that pays a monthly dividend. Make choices about your life based on the assumption of having money. Be grateful for the money you have, and remember that all your other money is just waiting for you to call it forth! Think wealthy to become wealthy.

- Emotions: Feel as though someone wonderful loves you and wants to lavish you with their affection. *Feel* lovable and worthy. Feel loving toward everyone you meet—strangers, friends, family, animals. Feel passionate about your art or your singing or your dancing and translate that passion into your sensuality. Just send out love from every pore—be a love machine. *Feel* love to attract love.

How does one adapt this to a life of Practical Conscious Creation? Here are some specific recommendations.

1. To attract love, you must vibrate love in all aspects of your life:

o   Self-love, self-respect, and self-appreciation

- • Take care of yourself and your health.

- • Treat yourself as a lover would—occasional gifts, pampering, and lots of affection.

- • Accept and love yourself for who you are and how you look.

- • Be your own best friend.

o   Be loving

- • Treat everyone around you with kindness and love—partners, lovers, friends, colleagues, co-workers, and so on.

- • Treat people you meet for the first time with compassion and kindness.

- • Go out of your way to be helpful and kind to others.

- • Accept people without judgment.

- • See and seek the divinity in all people.

- • Start your day cloaking yourself in love, lighting up all your cells with love, being love.

o   Act as if you are in love and you are a great partner in a relationship

- • If you are in a relationship, act as if you are in love and you may find your partner being more romantic and attentive.

- • If you are not in love or dating anyone, create that euphoric feeling inside yourself and act as if you are.

- • Be a great companion and an understanding and supportive friend, so that you can attract a partner who is the same way.

- • Be open to love coming to you in all ways from all sources; don't screen out anyone who doesn't fit your "criteria."

2. To enjoy happiness, be happy:

o   Let go of your worry and cares

- • Release worrisome thoughts.

- Move forward with optimism and a feeling of well-being.
- Assume all is well.

o   Consider your challenges learning opportunities

- View all challenges as opportunities and ways to learn.
- Assume that everything happens for a reason.
- Assume that everything is in divine timing.

o   Find wonder and beauty everywhere

- Look for the beauty in everything.
- Treat every day and every experience with the wonderment of a child.
- Appreciate all the wonderful sensations that engage your sight, touch, feel, hearing, smell and mind.

o   Spend time doing the things you love, being with the people you love

- Find work that makes you happy and if the overall job doesn't, find aspects that do!
- Be in nature, which makes almost everyone happy!
- Plan more time with the people who help make your spirit soar.
- Exercise! That always makes people feel refreshed.
- Participate in hobbies or acts of self-expression.
- Find healthy and soul-satisfying ways to serve others.
- Listen to music that makes you happy.

o   Just choose to be happy! Vibrate joy.

3. To be abundant, feel and act abundant:

o   Generally feel abundant

- Feel grateful for all you have.
- Feel enriched by what already enriches your soul, your home, your social environment, and your heart.

- Feel the wealth of what you are—talented, smart, gifted, kind, hard-working, intuitive—whatever your personal assets happen to be.

- Feel enriched by what is yet to come.

- Act as if money is already on its way: it's yours . . . it's just not yet in your bank account.

- Feel wealthy beyond measure!

o   Treat money as if it's your best friend

- Feel grateful for what is in your account, or how much you have down on your home, for retirement savings, for the paycheck you now receive . . . even if it's unemployment!

- Enjoy spending the money you have—even when you do small things like going to the movies.

- Enjoy what money allows you to do (buy gifts for your kids, attend a self-help seminar, donate to disaster relief).

- Enjoy paying your bills knowing you are contributing to helping someone else like yourself pay their bills, someone perhaps less fortunate than you. Command each dollar you spend to go out in the world, help someone else, and come back to you enriched.

- Bless each check that comes into your home or office—payroll check, tax return, payment for merchandise or services rendered, stock dividend, whatever!

- Be generous: Give away your money (even small increments) as if you were wealthy and had plenty to give!

o   Surround yourself with things that remind you of wealth or make you feel wealthy

- Dress up and feel elegant.

- Adorn your home with signs of wealth (I have a large glass emerald on my coffee table that reminds me of wealth, and I have lots of brass, which reminds me of gold.)

- Purchase a few quality items that make you feel you are moving up in the world, rather than lots of smaller things that are of lesser quality.

- Spend on a select few things that make you feel luxurious—for example—1,000-thread-count sheets, a monthly massage, a long weekend at a spa or a B&B, a special new rose for your garden.

- Put a $100 bill in your wallet. Never spend it. Just look at it as a reminder and allow it to attract more of them!

4. Be peaceful and in the flow:

o   Make time for connection

- Meditate so you can be open to your higher self and Source.

- Meditate or be in quiet place to clear your mind and just be in a state of peace.

- Consciously open the connection between you and Source, invite the divine light or golden cord, state your intention to be in alignment with God, allow in guidance and wisdom.

- Create and practice rituals that reinforce your awareness of connection to The Universe.

- Vibrate peace and peacefulness.

- Vibrate loving, open, accepting energy.

o   Let go of anger, anxiety, and fear

- Remember that everything that makes you react is not real—it's all in your head. Lower your blood pressure by not making anything a big deal.

- Reduce or eliminate the mind chatter.

- Eradicate your emotional triggers by doing the spiritual work that clears the emotional blocks from your past experiences and memories.

- Be flexible and allow change to occur without resistance. Go with the flow.

o   Trust the Universe

- Constantly remind yourself that the Universe is operating in your highest good.

- Let go of the need to control, and have confidence that the Universe is taking care of your needs. "Your needs are met if you believe they are being met."

- Let go of resistance. Be in a state of acceptance, confidence, optimism, and joy at how everything is working out perfectly.

- Follow the guidance and go with the flow.

- Delight in how things work out, and follow guidance to correct or learn from those things that are challenges. Either way, it's in your highest good.

- Vibrate trust.

o Open to your intuition

- Listen for guidance.

- Watch for signs.

- Go with your gut.

o Be in a state of Godliness

- Do what is right in your heart.

- Do what is right for the planet.

- Be conscious and aware.

- Be in oneness. Vibrate oneness.

- Do what you think God would do.

Your job—if you choose to accept it (remember *Mission: Impossible?*)—is to match your frequency with whatever you desire to draw in. So sit down and make a list of the top three things you wish to experience. Then create a corresponding action, thought, and emotional expression for each one of those desires.

Now go out and live it! Rev up those vibrations so that you can become a frequency broadcaster like no other! Just remember to apply this simple formula to everything you'd like to attract into your life. Be what you want to transform into, have, or possess. Vibrate what you desire! Call forth your future by energizing it and matching your frequency!

Practical Conscious Creation Tip No. 6

Labels for Conscious Living

As I write this, my eyes stop on the words that I have taped to my computer as a daily reminder of what I want to achieve. Peace, Serenity, Love, Joy, Surrender, Trust, Acceptance. Taping words to a computer may seem trivial to some people, but I find them a powerful reminder of the state of being that I want to cultivate. I use my little labeling machine to create these as a way to keep important thoughts front and center, since I spend so much of my day at my desk. They keep me on the right track! You may want to think about what state of being you would like to create in your life and then place words of aspiration in a place that you frequent much of the day—or that you see when you arise in the morning or go to bed at night. Words are a gateway to our subconscious. The more we make them conscious, the more we become what we state! Happy labeling!

Detachment: The Art of Letting Go Once You've Put in Your Order

In Conscious Creation, we often address the importance of being in a high-frequency state and stress the skill of visualization, but one topic that frequently doesn't receive its due is detachment.

Detachment is what should happen after you've put in your order to the Universe. It's not disinterest; it's that wonderful place of confidence that the Universe is working on delivering your order.

Failure to detach is the state of anxiousness—questioning if manifesting really works, wondering if the Universe really heard your request, being in a state of fear that it might not manifest, repeatedly putting in the order just to make sure that it "takes," or wanting something sooooooo much that you choke off the positive energy bringing it your way.

The Universe needs only one clear, well-envisioned request to put things in motion! So how do you keep your hand off the controls and detach?

1. **Assume it's a done deal.** Stand in the belief that all is well and everything is working in your favor to bring your intention to fruition. My friend and fellow conscious creation teacher, Anisa Aven (www.creatavision.com), reports: "My favorite conversation with the Divine usually sounds something like this:

   God, this "issue" is YOUR job and YOUR responsibility, not mine. Therefore, I'm handing it over to you. I will relax and listen for your Divine Guidance. I will prepare to receive my good and know that this is handled. I will remember that my ONLY responsibility is to be aware of the Divine Presence within as the ONLY source and supply for all my good. I accept that as a Divine Child of God it is truly impossible for me to have any wants, needs or unfulfilled desires. Therefore, God, thank you for taking care of this for me. It is done."

2. **Occupy yourself with other self-nurturing tasks.** One of the best ways to just let it go is to do some self-pampering while the Universe is at work. It distracts your mind from what you do not yet have and focuses it instead on the blessings of what you do have. Women: take a long, hot, slow bath in water infused with essential oils; get a massage; put lotion all over your body, have a facial, plan a girlfriend's night on the town, and so on. Men:

Practical Conscious Creation Tip No. 7

Vision Boards

Don't underestimate the power of a vision board to help you manifest your future! You can use magazines, glue sticks, and posterboard, or you can create one digitally. The important thing is that it should be an evolving process that allows you to add, subtract, or change as your vision changes and expands. It needs to be in a prominent place, where you can encounter it daily (maybe even your screen saver?) World-famous feng shui expert Marie Diamond (www.mariediamond.com) says that—based on your birth year—you have a specific success corner, relationship corner, health corner, and personal growth corner in your home. You may wish to visit her website to determine in which direction each of these lie for you. Then place your vision board in your success corner. Let your vision board inspire the unlimited imagination that will lead the way into your future!

listen to some relaxing music, play hoops with your friends, read a best-selling book, have a men's day at the local spa, and so on. Relax into letting your wish take its own course.

3. **Occupy yourself with serving others.** This is a surefire way to put your self-awareness on the back burner and focus on the gift of what you can do for others. It's a perfect signal to the Universe that you are indeed ready to receive whatever you requested, so no need to think about it anymore!

4. **Do a ceremonial sendoff for your wish.** It's fun to actually deliver your wish to the Universe symbolically, releasing it from your hands. Mail it to God in an envelope. Secure and release a white dove to carry your message for you. Sing your request and allow the music to fade. Burn a candle to its completion after stating your intention or wish. Put it in a bottle and send it to sea. You get the idea!

5. **Go about your business with a smile and a glow!** Know that you are deserving and it's on its way. The best way to smooth the path of its arrival is to be happy, wear a smile, and feel good about yourself, your life, and the realization of your desires.

Chapter 2

Everyday Life

Each day has the potential to be a turning point in your life. By employing Conscious Creation techniques throughout your workday and at home, you will discover the potent power to transform your daily existence into a sequence of large and small miracles of manifestation. Employ and enjoy!

Traveling the Conscious Creation Road

Okay, so you set your course for the year by sitting down and Consciously Creating your vision. Maybe you even wrote down your vision and intentions. However, now you are two or three months down the line and wham! You're already thrown off course. Something unexpected has come along and redirected you. I don't mind sharing that this is what happened to me. I started down one path and suddenly found myself somewhere else. What do you do when that happens? Do you get frustrated and give up? Do you just figure that your year is already shot? Do you lose faith with your ability to mold and create your future? Or do you take that as a message from the Universe to look closely at why things have not followed your intentioned path. Here are some factors to check:

- Could this new path actually work for your highest good if you eliminate your resistance? Have you considered that the Universe may have a better path for you?

- Examine what vibrations you are emanating. Could negative emotions and thoughts be repelling or leading you astray from your desired direction?

- Check your values and beliefs. Is what you are asking for truly in alignment with what you believe, what you think you deserve, what you have in your heart, what you value, or how you see yourself? (This is the one that tripped me up!)

- Are your emotions matching your thoughts? Do you think you want something but are afraid of the consequences or the cost?

- Are you just being impatient and the Universe is just taking a roundabout way to get you there? Is your impatience becoming an energy block?

- Do you distrust the process?

- Is there a learning opportunity that the Universe is putting smack in the middle of your intended path, something that you must take care of before you can advance?

When you have looked at all these things, get back on the path again. Keep your same vision or change your vision based on what you have learned. Reestablish your sense of optimism and faith. Find the right vibration to smooth the path and keep you moving forward—even if it is a little tiny bit off course! The Universe knows where you're going, even if you don't!

Practical Conscious Creation Tip No. 8

The Wishing Well for Your Growth

Remember what it's like to throw a coin in a wishing well, in the hopes that it will bring something wonderful back to you? That's putting your faith in the future, in a benevolent force watching over you. I've been thinking that maybe you can use those same coins as an investment in your future in a different way. Most of us have at least a dollar a day that we can stash away somewhere. What if we were to put that dollar toward some program of self-improvement? The point is that we often say we don't have the money for guided self-growth, but if you make a little investment every day—just like a wishing well—at the end of the year, you'll have at least $365, a nice little fund that can be used for special opportunities to free your spirit and your mind. So why not create a special "wishing well" savings bank just for investing in yourself—giving yourself a way to more than just wish yourself well, but make yourself well.

Choosing Our Future

As each of us takes on the mantle of Conscious Creator, we become aware of the thoughts we have let overtake us, the emotions that have previously ruled us, and the words we use to imprison ourselves. As newly birthed Conscious Creators, we learn that we can indeed counter these powerful negative forces by consciously willing ourselves to think, feel, and speak differently, to raise our personal frequency through choice.

And so we might find ourselves reframing our thoughts and words into far more positive statements of possibility, opportunity, faith, and confidence. Indeed, we often may discover affirmations to be a valuable tool in making these changes. Using a phrase such as "I am. . . " is a compelling practice that helps shift our world view and allows us to grow into who we want to become. We now also go about our daily lives declaring our positive intentions instead of focusing on the negative. We often say we "will" do something, or we "intend" to take action.

However, while these are all very important positive and valid steps toward becoming a Conscious Creator and Master Manifestor, there is one phrase that is even more powerful because it implies a conscious will. That is to say, "I choose to. . . "

By stating these simple three words, "I choose to. . . ," you are telling the Universe that you are taking responsibility for your actions, that you are deliberately going down this path, and you are signaling to the Universe that you wish to attract its help in reaching the preferred outcome.

For example, here are the kinds of statements that are powerful incentives for the Universe to help you achieve what you have selected:

- "I choose to" open my heart, be more compassionate, and look at everyone else with the knowledge that we are one.

- "I choose to" be more abundant in my giving and my receiving.

- "I choose to" be open to receive love, support, compliments, joy, respect, and wisdom.

- "I choose to" be healthier and more disciplined in my self-care.

- "I choose to" be more confident and willing to speak up for what I need in my job and in my relationships, but to do this with grace and consideration for others.

Practical Conscious Creation Tip No. 9

The Universe Keeps Knocking

It's always amazing to me that when the Universe wants to get the message to you, it'll keep trying till the message gets through. I had a perfect example of this recently. In attending several personal development seminars on Manifesting (yes, the teacher is always learning!), I had my feet put to the fire on a personal challenge/opportunity by not one but two different wisdom leaders. Both told me the very same message in the space of 10 days. The message was: Make a Decision, Commit Yourself, Write Down the Steps You Will Do, and Take Action. Stop dithering around and going halfway. Ouch! Pretty clear, isn't it!? Those teachers were just the messengers, but the Universe was the Source.

You will often discover similar messages coming from people you meet, as I did, or you may see signs, hear music, open to certain pages of books, or have encounters that all point you in a particular direction. Ignore these at your peril, as the Universe will keep upping the stakes until it gets your attention! So take the hint when the Universe comes knocking—open the door!

- "I choose to" release my fears and trust the Universe.

- "I choose to" make wiser choices about the people with whom I spend my time.

- "I choose to" eat only those foods today that are nutritious and in my highest good.

- "I choose to" love and respect myself today.

- "I choose to" express my emotions in a healthy and appropriate manner, so that they free me from imprisonment.

- "I choose to" have a positive and healthy relationship with my parents and to forgive them for their unconscious actions.

- "I choose to" be a powerful attractant for abundance, and to show the Universe I am worthy of its gifts.

- "I choose to" be more patient with my children today, regardless of how they behave and what I am doing at the time.

See how much more power these words produce? You are standing tall and proud when you make a choice that is right for you. Proclaim that choice! And when you do, two things happen: you are consciously aware that you have made a commitment that you must now live up to, and the Universe sees the seriousness of your intent and supports you.

Choose to choose! Show the Universe that you are truly conscious of your thoughts, emotions, and actions. Let your choice be your ticket to a life of your design.

Let Go of the Past Before You Bring It Into the Future

While the past holds great memories for us as human beings, it is also a minefield for many. That mental landscape is full of booby traps and other things waiting to ambush us. Our long-buried memories can often establish beliefs and behavior patterns that rule our lives, our relationships, and the way we navigate the world, even though we are unaware of them. Easily recalled memories are vivid because they remind us of painful experiences of rejection and hurt that forced us to unconsciously build elaborate walls to protect against future pain.

The past is a place where we often get stuck. When we allow it to dominate our thinking, our motivation and our actions—or even subliminally do these things—we are limited and constrained in our lives, mired right where we are. No matter how hard you try to step out of the muck, it always sucks you back in. The past is a dangerous place to live.

And here's where it even gets more scary: If you hold onto the past, you will bring it into the future.

If you are visualizing and vibrating the energy of the past, focusing on the negative past experiences in your life, you will manifest more of them in the future. By focusing on what went wrong or what displeased you, your energy will draw in more things that can go wrong in the future. If you are remembering all the slights and the rejections of old, you are destined to experience more slights and rejections in the future. That's what you are vibrating.

Remember: What you think, you create.

So leave your negative past at the door. If you want to create a vibrant, happy, unlimited future for yourself, you must start with today as the first day of creation. You must focus on happy, loving, fulfilling memories that enhance your life and that you can re-create in the future. Happy memories raise your personal frequency so that you can create more of the same going forward.

Or you can simply live with optimism and faith in a grand future, allowing it to unfold on your waves of positive energy. Don't burden the future with the negative energy and thoughts of the past. Let it be clean, open, and expansive. Release the future from anything that will bog it down and keep you stuck.

Here are a few steps you can take to sweep out those old memories, before they can infect your future:

1. **Catch yourself in the act.** Every time you find yourself wallowing in the past, zap the memory with your magic laser, disintegrating it. Now there is no negative memory to go back and retrieve.

2. **Scan your body for hidden negative memories.** Get into a quiet meditational state. Call up the memory, say thanks for all the protection it gave you, and release it, observing that it no longer serves you. You have to make room for your unlimited future. Then light some incense to symbolically burn away all the last remnants of it.

Practical Conscious Creation Tip No. 10

Are You Ready for a Shakeup?

Too often we find ourselves in a rut. We do the same things day in and day out. We eat the same foods. We think the same way. Our frequency just slides lower and lower as we feel stuck. I love the quote from Albert Einstein that says: "Insanity is doing the same thing over and over again, and expecting a different result." So what's the best way to break out of a rut? Do something radical and different! This doesn't mean you should change everything in your life, but just do one thing different. And keep doing it differently until you sense a change of energy. One shift can lead to other shifts. Remember: everything is connected. And before you know it, you're moving forward again with excitement and enthusiasm. You're out of the rut!

3. **Find out why you are hindered.** If you are feeling stuck and unable to move forward, go looking for the memory that may be keeping you where you are. Bring it out, look at it, reexperience the emotion that it creates, and then let go of it. Breathe deeply the whole time, expelling the memory from your DNA.

4. **Do a little scream therapy.** Go scream out the memory where no one can hear you. Get rid of it. Good riddance. No need to have it clutter the future.

5. **Forgive and ask for forgiveness.** An act of forgiveness will bring conclusion and closure to an open festering wound. Finish your business here so you can be healed.

6. **Set an intention to release unhealthy memories.** Setting an intention is like making a pact with the Divine. If you keep up your part of the bargain to live a life without wallowing in the past, the Universe will help you achieve it.

So move forward with joy and optimism, unhindered by the past. Go boldly into the future!

Fear: The Siren Call to Change

When most people think of fear, they conjure pictures of screaming women in slasher movies, horrible mindless villains, or heroes chased by zombies. But, for most of us, fear feels more like an insidious virus that our minds and emotions create to stop us from moving forward.

Fear is the mind/ego's way of saying "I'm not going there! I like being right where I am. I'm familiar with my current state. If I plunk myself right down here, nothing can hurt me because I already know this territory. I'm not worthy and if I stretch myself, I might get rejected."

Fear means you are not willing to venture into the unknown, not willing to take risk, not willing to accept and adjust to change. Fear is about ignoring imperatives to change, putting your head in the sand and expecting the problem to go away, allowing others to control your life because you may not have the courage or confidence to control your own. And fear always leaves your life messy, miserable, and myopic (limited in scope).

You may not actually be aware of the grip fear has over you. And even if you are, you sometimes feel powerless to change because of past, tightly held beliefs.

But fear can be your ally. If you feel it, it is a siren call to change!

When you bump up against fear, you know you are called to move forward, be bolder, take a well-calculated risk, flow with the change imposed on you, make the course correction you've been resisting, cross the seemingly impenetrable barrier, strike out on your own, act in your own self-interest, or reach for freedom!

So how can you move beyond it to something better when fear is at your door?

1. **The flipside of fear is faith.** If you are experiencing fear, then something is pressing you to change. Where does that urgency for change originate—in your heart, in your spirit, in the Universe? If it originates in the Universe, your heart and your spirit are indeed pushing you forward. Let go and trust. Allow your faith to spring forward. Ask if this change is in your highest good. If the answer is "yes," then trust the Universe to allow the benefits to unfold once you give up resisting and start moving forward. If the pressure is mounting from outside—job loss, relationship breakup, and so on—again ask if this is in your highest good? These conditions are the Universe speaking to you in the dialect of "loving change and redirection." Trust and go with the flow.

2. **Affirming "I am FEAR-LESS!"** Whenever I get overwhelmed by fear, I repeat this affirmation again and again. I repeat it with power as if I were brandishing a wooden stake in order to ward off a vampire! My confidence grows and the fear lessens as I remind myself that I have no reason to fear because I am a fearless being with the Ultimate Support System!

3. **Get clear.** If part of your fear is confusion about what steps to take or where to head, spend time in silence asking questions. Reach out to someone else who can coach you through the process of getting clear or put your options in writing. These are just some of the ways you can get focused, so that with clear intention you can begin loosening the grip of fear.

4. **What is the worst thing that could happen if you do move forward?** Usually you will have built up this fear into something greater than it could possibly ever be in reality. When you really look at the worst thing that could happen, it's usually not all that terrible. Then it's a simple realization

that moving forward easily outweighs your realistic worst-case scenario. Voilà, paralysis unblocked!

5. **Bring it out into the light.** The more you look at fear from an objective standpoint, as if you were not in your body—bring it out, hold it to the light, examine why it's making you crazy—the more power you have to eradicate the fear of it you are harboring. Think of yourself as the sleuth bringing the clues out into the open so you can solve the case.

6. **Recalibrate your limiting beliefs and go for expansion.** Look at the beliefs that are causing you to hold onto your fear. What's real, what's not? Make a list of these limiting concepts. Then list the opposite possibility—the expansionist and unlimited belief that you could be holding—the one that would enable you to move forward with confidence and courage.

7. **Stop thinking about what you're giving up and start looking at what you are potentially gaining.** What's the upside? This is an easy one! Ultimately moving toward your highest good will always have a greater potential upside than staying where you are, or giving up what you currently have.

8. **Talk it out.** Find a forward-thinking and positive friend, someone who is used to stepping through fear, or perhaps a counselor or coach. Talk about what you are feeling. Ask that person to tell you stories of how he or she found success by moving beyond fear. Be inspired by other people's courageous acts.

9. **Fear is just thoughts and emotions—those can be changed!** Fear is just something you created in your mind. It is not real. It is simply a virtual prison that you can choose to make disappear by hitting the delete button!

10. **Stop clinging and start living—embrace the unknown!** Life is an exciting e-ticket ride with everything you want if you will simply embrace the unknown. But if you persist on clinging to the known, you'll never experience it. Greet the unknown future with a warm welcome and magical things start to happen.

11. **Consciously create/visualize the outcome.** Once you release fear and unwaveringly commit to change, you can help secure a positive future by Consciously Creating it. Make sure you are operating in a high frequency, create your visualization, postmark it to the Universe and then let it go with a blessing of gratitude! Fear has a way of fading in the wake of action and purpose.

Practical Conscious Creation Tip No. 11

Music

Music is a window into the soul and a way to prepare yourself to receive. I find that whenever I turn on my favorite instrumental music—either New Age or soft jazz—I can actually feel my blood pressure reduce and the stress drain out of me. If music has this same effect on you, it is helping to put you in a receptive frame of mind for your two-way communication with the Universe. If you take the time to just relax and listen, rather than busy yourself with activities, music can help you open yourself to messages from the Universe, clear your energy blocks, and alter your brain wave pattern so that you are a more effective sender-receiver of positive high frequency energy—the energy that speeds manifestation. So next time you put on something restful and beautiful to listen to, give yourself the quiet time to fully allow its magic to work on you.

12. **Remember who you are!** You are an unlimited being with a mandate to live in joy. Fear has no place in your abundant, richly rewarded life of service to the planet.

All Things Are Possible

I wish I had a dollar for every person who said, "I can't," "That won't happen," "It's impossible," or "That's beyond me." I'd be the proverbial very rich woman!

It's truly amazing how we short-change ourselves by thinking from a place of limitation and failure even before we attempt something.

So let me give you a little newsflash: All things are possible!

Wouldn't it be amazing if we simply started our problem-solving and creative thinking from this premise? Instead of focusing on all the reasons why something can't happen.

Are you a negative problem solver or a positive problem solver? Do you eliminate all the optimal solutions from the start as being too improbable or having too many obstacles, and just live with whatever is convenient, easy, or just adequate? Do you pick your job this way or your spouse? You don't deserve what you really want or are not worthy of it, so you will "settle?"

Or do you start by believing the optimum is possible and then marshal all the support you can to make it so? Do you believe that your belief can help it manifest? Do you hold the faith that the Universe will open amazing doors if you trust in the most positive outcome and begin working toward it?

All things are possible. World peace is possible. We may not have it yet, but it is possible. If we stop believing, we stop trying. Personal abundance and prosperity is possible. If you believe that, then it's just a matter of figuring out how to get there. A wonderful, loving relationship is possible—if not with the person you are currently involved with, then with someone else. Inner peace and joy are possible. You just need to ask the right questions and follow the guidance.

Believe in the possibility of the possible. Believe in your unlimited power to consciously create. Look at the infinite instead of the finite. Start moving forward with the highest goal in mind, and look for avenues that will take you

Practical Conscious Creation Tip No. 12

What People Think of You is None of Your Business

I recently read this statement in one of those circulars going around the Internet, and I thought, "now isn't that a wonderful way to say that the only discernment that should mean anything to you is your own!" If you find yourself always wondering what other people think of you or whether you are "acceptable" in their eyes, then learn this mantra: "What other people think of me is none of my business!" Live your life as if it was open to no one's judgment! Your life just is. Become the best *you* that you can be and let go of the desire to gain other people's approval. You'll find great freedom in choosing to mind your own business!

there. If you don't reach the pinnacle, it might just be that where you end up is exactly where you should be—but you didn't get there by "settling." You got there by striving and setting your sights high. Your personal satisfaction level will be significantly greater.

By holding the optimistic philosophy that all things are possible, you create the energy for great outcomes. Your positive vibrations will continue to attract those wonderful possibilities that you desire—and some you didn't even expect!

So when you catch yourself saying, "I can't. . . " or "It won't. . . ," rewind and say, "Anything is possible" with enthusiasm and belief! And leave the door open for the seemingly "impossible" to become possible!

Doing the Difficult

Life would be so much better if everything was easy. But the reality is that only some things are easy; other things are easy, but we make them hard by the way we view them; and other things are simply difficult.

The easy things are a snap! You just do them and are done with it. You may even look forward to doing them.

The things that are easy but that we make difficult are another story. These are tasks to which we assign value—we give them an emotional charge. Such responsibilities may not be physically demanding, complicated, or time consuming—we just dread them or don't want to do them for some reason. The solution to these tasks is to simply take away the negative judgment and then recognize them for what they are: easy tasks that should require little of your energy but a lot of your focus and commitment. Eliminate the emotional charge, and they may even become a pleasure to accomplish because they really are not taxing. Think Snow White—"Whistle While You Work!"

Now for the difficult things. These are the tasks that people avoid tackling and delay until they no longer have a choice. We all hate to deal with confrontation, problems, and the unpleasant issues before us. But avoiding such matters is not just a real-world problem; it's an energetic block. If you fail to deal with problems through avoidance, the Universe will simply send the problem back to you in other ways, or create stagnancy in another area of your life.

"Doing the difficult" is as much a spiritual as physical and mental act. It requires making choices and moving forward with confidence that you may not always know the exact right answer but you will be guided along in a positive direction. Failure to move forward is surely the most self-destructive form of nonaction to which you can subject yourself. Once you take action, you will be rewarded by greater wisdom and even sometimes by unexpected assistance.

Here are some suggestions for dealing with "Doing the Difficult:"

- **Face your difficult tasks and confrontations with courage and resilience!** Personally, I like to tackle them first, rather than last, so that I can eliminate the heavy emotional toll of constantly having them in the back of my mind, knowing the unwanted task is still ahead. Once I get it done, I know I can look forward to something more pleasurable afterward.

- **Be prepared.** When you are prepared, you alleviate much of the anxiety. Whether this is doing advance research, pre-interviewing people, writing a plan, creating a presentation, "pre-running" the task in advance, or just rehearsing it in your mind, you will feel much more confident in a positive outcome once you have gotten "all your ducks in a row."

- **Ask for guidance . . . on all levels!** This might involve looking toward a mentor or coach to "try out" your thinking. Or it might be asking the Universe to provide knowledge, wisdom, and the right answers to a dilemma. Ask for what you need, then simply get quiet and listen for answers. But don't be impatient, because those answers may not come until the precise moment you need them.

- **Envision the task being easy.** The more energy you put toward envisioning it being easy, the more likely it will be! Start with the assumption that the task is easier than you think it will be!

- **Don't anticipate conflict.** If you go into a situation anticipating conflict, you are increasing the odds that there will be. Remember: *What you think, you create.* So hold a vision and assumption that there is no conflict—only differing points of view—and that all parties will eventually come to a consensus that serves everyone well.

- **Take your emotions out of it.** Eliminate the dread or the fear that goes along with performing the task. These emotions in themselves make whatever you are facing more difficult and unpleasant, and in true Conscious Creation fashion will attract more obstacles. Assign no emotional value to whatever you are doing—it's just something that must be accomplished,

Practical Conscious Creation Tip No. 13

Keep an Affirmations Log

Affirmations are a powerful way to generate positive energy and raise your personal frequency. They help you change your core beliefs and open you to growth. Keeping a log or compendium of affirmations has several purposes:

1. It reminds you to affirm these statements daily and to have them all in one place so you don't forget any of them.
2. It keeps them in a place where you will always find them.
3. It allows you to add new ones that you create or obtain from other sources or subtract those you have outgrown.
4. If you keep all of them, it provides a record of your growth and how you have evolved.

There are several simple ways to create your log. One is to simply keep a list on your computer or handwritten in a diary or notebook. Another is to develop an audio compilation in the event you wish to listen to your own voice repeat them as a daily "mantra." To accomplish this, you may consider purchasing a small digital recorder which you can use to transfer the file to an iPod or your laptop. Other options include setting up a recording program directly on your computer if you have a speaker/mic. The free audio dashboard at www.audacity-sourceforge.net allows you to create high quality MP3 files at your desk. You can also register for an inexpensive account at Audio Acrobat (audioacrobat.com) where you can record affirmations over the phone, then download the results to your computer before transferring them to a digital player. Lastly, you can log on to www.theaffirmationspot.wordpress.com, which has hundreds of prerecorded affirmations. Play these each day when you rise, go to sleep, or when you are exercising.Happy Affirming!

and nothing more. As Nike® says, "Just do it!"

- **Ask for help, gather your support.** Nowhere does it say in your life contract that you have to do everything *alone*! Be willing to ask for help and support, so that perhaps a difficult task can be made easier through the assistance of others—and more pleasant by simply having the joy of sharing a task with people you enjoy. Remember Snow White again and her little string of helpers. . .

- **Commit focused time.** One of the best ways to make a difficult task more difficult is by continually being diverted. People with attention deficit disorder are prime examples of people who are distracted from finishing the task at hand and create even more anxiety as things don't get done. So just make sure that you start this task with a clear schedule, and commit that nothing should divert or distract you from focusing on completion.

- **Choose to enjoy the experience, or be happy to be accomplishing it.** Get rid of that big cloud of negativity. Go into the task with a positive, happy attitude, knowing that you are fulfilling whatever is being asked of you by the Universe, and that you are stepping up to the plate spiritually, emotionally, physically, and mentally. You're clearing your emotional blocks by taking responsibility and choosing to do the "right thing"—whatever that might be. By "Doing the Difficult" with grace and empowerment, you are growing in experience, knowledge, and wisdom.

How Old Will You Be When. . . ?

Every year, while coaching and mentoring individuals or groups on Conscious Creation, I hear some folks lament that they are getting older and have not followed their dreams. And the older they get, the more fearful they are that they will never do whatever it is that ignites their passion. Time is slipping away and they haven't even started toward their heartfelt goal.

When I hear these sad refrains, I tell them a favorite story. Many years ago, I read an item in the Dear Abby column. A woman in her 60s wrote to Dear Abby saying that she had always wanted to go to law school. She was torn over whether she should even start school at that age—she would be so much older than the other students, she was nearly old enough to collect social security, and so on. "Should I do it? I'll be 64 when I graduate," she asked the columnist.

Dear Abby's response was classic. "But of course you should do it. How old would you be in four years if you didn't do it?"

The answer always made me laugh. We'll be the same age if we don't follow our hearts, but we'll be a lot less fulfilled!

So what are you denying yourself because you might be too old, too tired, too different from everyone else, too embarrassed, too ashamed, too foolish, too busy, too fearful, or too poor?

What are you yearning to do that you haven't?

- Complete a degree in school?
- Go back for advanced training in some skill?
- Start a treasured hobby?
- Learn a skill passed on from your parent or grandparent?
- Take cooking classes?
- Have Lasik surgery so you can get rid of your glasses?
- Rescue a puppy or kitten and taken it into your home?
- Start your own business?
- Begin a martial arts class?
- Sign up for an online dating service?
- Start training for a marathon?
- Take flying lessons?
- Have a baby?
- Write a book? Start a speaking career?
- Travel around the world, around the country? See the national parks?
- Ask out someone that you've always admired from afar?
- Study a foreign language?
- Do a night of stand-up comedy?
- Sail around the Caribbean?
- Drop everything and try your hand at an acting career?
- Move out of the house?

Practical Conscious Creation Tip No. 14

Taking the Pressure Off—Giving in to Divine Timing

Do you ever get to the point when you feel you're a tea kettle about to boil over because you are under pressure from so many deadlines? Here's what I do. When I get stressed and worried about the limited time I have to get something accomplished based on deadlines that I imposed on myself or that have been imposed on me—and perhaps I'm stuck waiting on other people—I sit back and say, "Trust the Universe. It'll come together in my highest good." Then I remind myself, "It may not be my timing, but it'll be in divine timing." And that takes the worry and control off my shoulders . . . and, of course, then everything happens just as it should.

- Become a teacher?

- Plant a garden and grow your own vegetables?

- Have a fling with an old flame who is single again?

- Change career so that you are serving others?

- Give yourself a week at a health spa, away from the kids?

- Buy a ticket to the World Series, an NBA Final, the Super Bowl or the Masters?

- Take up painting, or dance, or yoga, or playing a musical instrument?

- Or any other passion that has eluded you. . .

If you recognize yourself in any of these questions, then you should begin seriously thinking about the value of your time on this planet. Denial is a misuse of your spiritual capital. Go and be what you truly desire to be. You are denying your destiny.

Use your skills of Conscious Creation to manifest whatever it is you need to move forward to support your plan and desire. Consciously Create the time, the resources, the opportunity, the mentor or the courage to move forth. But mostly focus on the goal—what you want to be doing—and let the Universe fill in the "how." Take action. Step out, sign up, start moving. After all, how old will you be if you don't follow your heart?!

Freedom from Guilt

Oftentimes when we think of negative frequencies that keep us mired in unhappy, unsatisfying lives, we point to fear, anger, hatred, revenge, and jealousy—strong, powerful emotions. But there is one negative frequency that most people forget. It's just as poisoning, because it's one we inflict on ourselves: guilt.

Guilt is defined in the dictionary as a feeling of responsibility, remorse, or regret for some offense, crime, wrong, and so on—"whether real or imagined."

Guilt seems benign. Nobody need know about it but you. You can hide it well. You can bury it. You can even be unaware that you have it. But guilt is insidious. It makes you feel worthless and unworthy. It may prevent you from playing the role you are destined to play in the world because you're afraid of "being found out." Guilt allows others to manipulate and enslave you. It certainly stymies your ability to be a Conscious Creator, keeping you mired in low-frequency vibrations, rather than the positive high frequencies that allow you to manifest effectively and to lead a happier, struggle-free life of your own direction.

You might be feeling guilty over what you "aren't" or for what you did or didn't do. It could be over your complicity in someone else's downfall. Perhaps you're experiencing guilt for not speaking up on behalf of someone else—or for yourself. Your guilt may be about your failure to please another—your boss, your spouse, your children, or your parents. It could be over lies told, promises broken, or integrity shattered. Maybe you feel guilty for errors of judgment, relationships that you torpedoed, people you let go out of your life that you now regret. Or perhaps you just feel guilty for not being a better person—one who does not judge and loves unconditionally.

Whatever reasons you have to justify feeling guilty, they are illusory, unnecessary, and unproductive. You don't need to spend your life punishing yourself for acts you felt were wrong—real or perceived. By holding onto guilt you cannot live fully—it's like being truncated, held down, or tethered. You cannot fly if you are still anchored to the earth. When you release guilt and open yourself for forgiveness and renewal—and allow the Universe to salve your wounds—you can begin to sprout wings. You can move forward in freedom and create positive new experiences that are unburdened by guilt and remorse.

Here are nine steps you can take to release guilt and elevate your spirit:

1. **Look at the issue with objective eyes.** Is this really your problem? Is it real or imagined? Is this truly your responsibility? Put it in perspective. Is this really worth worrying about? If you were to look back in a year, would anybody really care?

2. **Examine what fear this guilt masks.** What do you fear you will lose? If you look at the worst-case scenario, it's probably not half as bad as your imagination manufactures. What really can be taken from you if you value and believe in yourself?

3. **If the guilt is caused by something that might be healed or changed, step up and try to correct the situation or apologize.** Look for a middle ground or solution. Your overtures may be accepted or they may not, but you have taken the right step to try to resolve it.

Practical Conscious Creation Tip No. 15

Animal Magnetism

Animals are a great source of inspiration in your Conscious Creation process. And they are a wonderful trigger for your visioning process. For example, if you see a hawk drifting over you, then envision yourself flying free, wafting over the air streams, with nothing to hold you down. Give yourself the sensation of being totally uplifted and without worry. Breathe into it and let your emotions soar. Puppies and kittens embody unconditional love and playfulness, traits that we all long to enhance in our lives. Bunnies (like the white cottontails we have here in my neighborhood) represent lovableness and curiosity. Butterflies should trigger the essence of graceful beauty. As you encounter creatures in the animal kingdom, allow them to inspire your visions of Conscious Creation to heighten the feelings and the traits you desire to instill in your life.

4. **Then you *must* forgive yourself.** This is the most essential step in the process. It's okay to acknowledge errors or mistakes made in the past, but if you set a new course through your intentions and actions, you deserve forgiveness from yourself. And, of course, the Universe will demonstrate forgiveness once you have shown love and respect for yourself.

5. **Let go of the past.** Don't hold onto the negative vibrations or negative memories. Experience the emotion, wrap it up in a shiny balloon and imagine it being lifted out of sight into the galaxy where it is transmuted. And then deliberately and intentionally release the burden of guilt. Imagine taking off the yoke and walking away unbowed.

6. **Build new bridges and create a new pattern of behavior.** When you consciously change your behavior to live with integrity in your actions and relationships, you generate new karmic energy. Present the authentic "new you" as you go forward in life and create new relationships. Don't mourn the old ones; just see them as a learning experience.

7. **Make wise choices so you won't have a reason to feel guilty.** Use your best judgment going forward. Look at the long-term consequences of your actions, and weigh all the considerations *before* committing yourself. This doesn't mean that everything will be perfect, but it does mean that your "right action" has set an intention for a course that is healthy for you, others, and the world. You have created a situation where you know you've done your very best.

8. **Vigilantly watch for signs of guilt and take steps to eradicate it.** Zap guilt like you would an annoying gnat. If you feel it coming on, look back and go through the steps above.

9. **Release and live free of guilt.** Give yourself a break! You deserve to live guilt-free. Make an intention to never return to the yoke of guilt. Focus on the life ahead and living it with joy and freedom.

What Must I Become?

Most of us live a life filled with regret about what we are not. We castigate our-selves for falling short, for not being a better person, or for not being more suc-cessful. We look at others and aspire to be like them. We would like to be a better relationship partner, a better parent, a more compassionate person, a more ambitious individual, a better-educated person, a more intuitive individ-ual, a more gifted businessperson, a better caregiver, a more patient individ-ual… The list goes on and on.

So rather than contemplate what we are not (which of course attracts more of that which we don't want to be), why not set out to ask and establish *What must I become?*

This is a key question, one that can really shift your focus. It's not about what you can achieve. It's not about what you can acquire. It's about becoming someone who has a higher resonance in the Universe, someone who can be a more perfect and fulfilling YOU!

By really thinking through this question you can begin to create a template for the complete person into whom you want to evolve. We know that one must have a clarity of vision in order to create and attract the support for it. By con-templating the question *What must I become?*, you can generate a full picture of where you are headed—and gain universal support for your striving to be-come that person. You can't just depend on the Universe; you must take action. But answering this question is the first step in becoming the unlimited person that you want to be.

Step One: Sit down with a computer or a pen and write this question at the top of the page: WHAT MUST I BECOME?

Step Two: Now break this down farther:

• **What general traits would I like to develop, improve, or enhance to grow as a self-realized, mature, and responsible person?** Think about where you have fallen short in the past. Perhaps explore where you have become emotional or out of control? Certainly for me, patience is my number one quest for myself, and I know this to be true for many others. What about letting go of judgment? Handling anger differently? Being more positive, hopeful, and upbeat? Being more trusting or more tactful and thoughtful? Being kinder? Being more generous and grateful? No doubt you can think of many traits you'd like to improve.

- **To whom would I like to relate better and what part can I play in that?**
Parents, children, spouse, boyfriend, girlfriend, lovers, boss, people I work with or supervise, friends, teachers or mentors, clerks at stores, waiters, neighbors, people who want something from me, people in need, and so on. . .

- **What habits or traits would I like to develop to create greater inner peace?**
Calmness under pressure? Acceptance of how things are instead of how I want them to be? A daily practice of meditation or tai chi or qi gong? More reading time for spiritual books? More reflection time? Release of my need to always be right or have the last word? Forgiving anyone with whom I am angry? More physical activity? What else?

- **What traits can I develop to be more successful professionally?** Better focus? Better people skills? Punctuality? Less time on the Internet and more networking? Study other successful professional people? Reach out to a coach or mentor? Release myself from the "I have to do it all or it won't be right" syndrome? Learn new professional skills you've been resisting? Be more willing to share? Better money management? More willing to get expertise from others? You get the idea.

- **What would I like to change about how I look at and treat myself?** Be more forgiving? Be less critical? Be more patient and tolerant? Be more nurturing and compassionate? Be willing to receive help? Be more openhearted and loving?

Step Three: From these, create a picture of WHAT I WILL BECOME. Write a full description of you as the person who embodies all of these qualities.

Step Four: Now make a list of actions that you will take to move yourself toward becoming the individual you have pictured.

Step Five: Implement your list of actions.

By focusing your mind, your attention, and your time on willing yourself to be a new-and-improved you, you can go from WHAT MUST I BECOME? to WHAT I AM! May the process be easier and more effortless than you can imagine!

Practical Conscious Creation Tip No. 16

The Power of Water

Water is a great conductor of positive spiritual energy. Have you ever found, like I have, that some of your best ideas come while taking a shower? Another friend of mine reports that when she's having a negative day or experience, she goes in and washes her hands extensively, finding that her cares seem to go away with the suds. I love the sound of running water, or water trickling in a fountain or a creek. It calms me and creates a kind of alpha state that lets me relax and allow in positive energy. In feng shui, it is said that having a fountain in front of your door attracts not only positive energy but abundance, too! However, my absolute favorite way to "soak up" the positive energy of water is to immerse myself in it—in either a bathtub or a pool. I am fortunate to have a pool in my backyard and I just love to get in and go neck deep in water, allowing myself to simply bob and float in the water and feel its gentle caress. If you can spend more time in and around water, I think you will find a tremendous sense of peace and joy, regardless of whatever else is going on in your life. It's the perfect way to raise your personal vibration.

Power Pronouncements

So many of us live in a place of hesitancy about our lives. We're not exactly sure we are who we want to be. We're not really clear on what we want or where we wish to go. We're not convinced we really deserve what we desire. We might be beaten up by childhood experiences of a failed relationship, so we are afraid to go boldly into the world. We often do the shuffle and the two-step so that we don't have to really make a stand . . . that might be risky and terrifying. People might figure out we're a fraud!

Aha! But let me clue you in. Hesitancy is a curse. Remember: He who hesitates is lost! Being neither here nor there means that you are not fully alive. You're in a state of limbo that doesn't allow you to grow. To grow means that you must throw off the fear and the reluctance, and actually take a stand!

Even if you are not yet sure of where you are headed or what you have to do to advance or who you yet want to be, you can begin to grow by declaring *what you know to be true and what you want to be true!* I call these Power Pronouncements! Consider them affirmations on steroids!

It's time you shed your cloak and come out into the light. Declare yourself!

- **I am. . .** (intuitive, beautiful, sexy, honest, good-looking. Courageous, fearless. . .)

- **I will be. . .** (healthy before the end of this year, cruising financially, passionate about my new job, on top of the pile on my desk next week, loving my life, finding romance. . .)

- **I know that. . .** (I am loved by God, I am loved by my employees, I am capable of learning the latest version of this software, I am clever enough to lead this team to success, I can develop a successful healing practice with the skills I already have. . .)

- **I feel. . .** (powerful, strong, smart, gifted, talented, willing, enthused, excited, emboldened, inspired. . .)

- **I am a. . .** (great business person, talented singer, fantastic office manager, superior waiter, spiritually conscious and connected person. . .)

Get the idea? Sit down and make a list of the Power Pronouncements that resonate with you personally, and address the areas where you do indeed feel "weak" or "unfulfilled." These are the areas that need shoring up! Break these

Practical Conscious Creation Tip No. 17

Savor the Magic

Sometimes we forget that there is magic in our lives. It's all around us. It's in the sound of wind chimes. It's in the giggle of a child. It's in the rich color of roses. It's in the smile of a stranger. It's in the smell of incense. It's in the chemistry between two people. Don't forget to savor the magic! Your life becomes infinitely better when you open to the rapture and delight of mystery and magic. You'll find your frequency rise and your manifesting become equally magical.

declarations down into each of the previous five categories (I am, I will be, I know, I feel, I am a. . .) based on what you aspire to be, do, and experience.

Once you've done that, do the following:

Step One: Say these into the mirror or yell them out loud in your backyard.

Step Two: Declare them boldly and courageously to a friend, spouse, or partner. Yes, this means you have to abandon your anonymity and really risk embarrassing yourself! But here's the good part, by stating these things before others and God, you are more than halfway committed to believing them and making them come true! You're increasing the odds that you can in fact manifest what you have stated! Begin believing that you are what you declare.

Step Three: When you've practiced and gained your confidence, you are truly ready to reveal your new and powerful self. GO SAY THESE POWER PRO-NOUNCEMENTS TO A CROWD!

You can do it. You really are who you declare yourself to be. Or you are at last on the way there!

Inspiring Inspiration

Ahhh. . . *Sweet Inspiration!* Remember that song from the 1960s? Inspiration is indeed sweet. It's the wellspring of our hearts, and the gateway to our unique and fulfilling future. It is the manner in which we create what is distinctly unique about ourselves.

So here are some important questions to ask yourself:

- What inspires me?
- How do I inspire myself?
- Where does my inspiration originate?
- How can I inspire more inspiration in my life?
- Where can I apply it?
- What can it do for me?

Inspiration, the great problem solver, is the source of ideas that help us change and correct our lives when they just aren't working. It's the artistic expression when our souls are yearning to communicate or release our emotions and extol our love of beauty. Imagination represents that connection to the Universe that brings forth newness—a breakthrough, something amazing! It's you co-creating with the Universe.

Where can you see inspiration at work in your life?

Business: Inspiration can lead you to start a new business, revitalize an old one, create more appealing advertising and marketing tools, invent new products, develop unique and novel marketing niches, create innovative ways to motivate staff, mold a new job that's just right for you, develop a speaking platform that is different from all others, find alternative distribution options, develop creative breakthroughs in positioning your product or business, communicate in new ways with your clientele and reignite their interest.

Relationships: Inspiration can be the key to returning the romance to your partnership and be the door-opener for more creativity in designing your relationship. It will lead you to new places to find a relationship partner. Inspiration allows you to reinvent yourself so that you are attracting a different kind of partner, one that is more connected to your Higher Self. And spur you to create positive inspired ways to communicate more effectively and with greater love.

Home: Inspiration helps you to manifest the perfect home environment—indoor and outdoor. It can direct you to the right place for your personal sanctuary and what needs to be there for you to allow your soul to settle in comfortably. Your inspiration will imbue your home with your light and your distinctive touch so that guests recognize your residence as a beautiful reflection of you.

Artistic Expression: Inspiration enables you to create from deep within your heart and your soul connection. Whatever your spirit wants to celebrate, express, or release can be seen through your artistic expression. Whether that is art, photography, dance, music, song, design, or other forms of self-expression, artistic expression is an essential outlet for everyone.

Playtime/Hobbies: Inspiration can be seen in what you choose to collect, make, create, cook, grow, craft, assemble, build, participate in, or where you choose to travel. Your playtime is your childlike inspiration manifest in your adult life.

Inspiration is an imperative for a healthy life. Each of us needs both the influence of it in our daily existence and the expression of it.

So how does one inspire more inspiration?

- Put aside time for it. Make time each week to tap into your creative connection, however you are inspired.

- Meditate or quiet your mind so that you are open to the inspiration that comes to you when the noise is screened out.

- Listen to music that stirs your soul.

- Go places that give you creative inspiration from other art forms: art galleries, design studios, car shows, boutiques and stores with unique merchandise, festivals and fairs, museums, other artists' studios, and so on.

- Find a place in nature that inspires you. The ocean, a meadow, a forest, a waterfall, the desert, a flower garden, a butterfly sanctuary, and so on.

- Surround yourself with pictures of beauty—taken from magazines, posters, photography, the Web, digital slide shows, paintings, calendars, and so on.

- Change your home to be inspirational. Find the books, candles, images and other items that create the mood for you to call forth your creative side.

- Go on a spiritual retreat or to a spiritual center of divinity such as the Self-Realization Fellowship in Pacific Palisades in California, a place carefully designed for you to open yourself to universal messages and connection.

- Help someone else in their creative endeavor (redecorating their home, for instance), which will give you ideas for your own life.

- Collaborate with others in creative undertakings (such as a mural or collage) because two or more people can inspire each other.

- Find a teacher or mentor who will help you unlock your creativity.

Don't overlook the role of inspiration in your life. And remember that as you are inspired, you inspire others! Let your inspirational light shine!

Practical Conscious Creation Tip No. 18

Give Yourself a Time Out!

In the hustle and bustle of daily life, there are undoubt-edly times when the stress level gets to you. You can be-come cranky, moody, demanding, tearful, angry, or frustrated. Now before you do something rash and you let your frequency come crashing down, take a time out! Just like parents send their children to their room, do something to create a break from whatever is stressing you. Go outside for a few minutes; have a soda, juice, or frozen coffee drink; take a nap; do a few exercises; start a quiet meditation with a mantra ("I am at peace and all is well"); call someone who brings a smile to your face; write an email to someone you love; go buy a book; light a candle and set an intention; listen to your heartbeat, sing a few bars of your favorite song, or catch some tunes on your iPod. Give yourself 20 minutes before you get back in the game!

The Magic of Changing Your Perspective

For most of us, dealing with changes and events that move us out of our comfort zone instantly takes us to a place of fear and negative thinking. It is the rare person who doesn't emotionally invest the experience with anxiety and assign a negative value to it.

Yet the truth is that all things are neutral, *they just are*—until we lend our perspective to them and assign value. More importantly, every experience brings with it an opportunity for growth—for greater wisdom, for new knowledge, for redirection from the Universe, or for expansion in some way, shape or form.

The task for us as Conscious Creators is to retrain ourselves not to immediately go to that dark place, but instead to seek the light and—assign *positive* value to every experience. The best way to do that is to learn new perspectives, and to apply them to each situation. You can magically turn a perceived problem into a blessing by asking the right questions or applying the right filter.

Let's expand our thinking and open up to the many new ways to look at things. By having these "tools" in your tool kit, testing the ones that work best for you, then applying them through practice many times over, you will be able to change your knee-jerk negative pattern of thinking to a welcoming and positive perspective that raises your frequency. And eventually will become your new permanent pattern of perspective.

Here are some really insightful questions that will lead you to look at your perceived challenges, problems, and issues as your next opportunities, gateways, and gifts:

- What is the joy to be found here?

- What is really great about this?

- What can I learn from this experience?

- How can I apply this in the future?

- How does this ultimately serve me?

- What is the upside to this experience?

- What is the takeaway here?

- What message is the Universe offering me?

Practical Conscious Creation Tip No. 19

Dress As If. . .

Let's say you don't feel very attractive this week. And you're used to going around in a ratty old pair of jeans and a decade-old top. You're in the dumps and life doesn't seem real abundant right now. How to dump the funk? *Dress as if . . . you're a million bucks!* Don't leave the house without putting on appealing clothes, full makeup, jewelry, a jaunty hat, a sexy scarf, your nicest boots. . . whatever makes you feel fantastic! It doesn't matter if you are just going to the mall, a mixer or the mailbox. Dress up and Consciously Create a feeling of being wealthy, well-cared for and charismatic. As you feel better about the face you are showing to the world, the more the world will show you the face of welcome, opportunity, and love. Strut your stuff!

- How can I turn this experience into something positive?

- What is the underlying truth about this experience—what is the reality without my emotional charge?

- What is the good that can come from this?

- Who can I help with this wisdom, knowledge, and experience?

- Where is this experience directing me?

- What is the invitation here?

- What new opportunity does this open up?

- How can I grow from this?

- Where is my expansion in this?

- What is this calling me to let go?

- What burden is being lifted through this experience?

- What deep calling within me wants expression through this change—even though it may be subconscious?

You undoubtedly know that everything happens for a reason. Here's an opportunity to look at that reason as Source does. You would not be offered this experience if there was not purpose here for you, your life, and your spiritual growth. But the Universe gives you these experiences out of its desire to help you reach your own truth and highest good. Use these questions for a more objective view of what is in your highest good.

Expectation is the Death of Serenity

I recently read a profound statement in Dr. Joy Browne's best-selling book, *Getting Unstuck*. She said: "Expectation is the death of serenity."

Whew! How true that is!

Just think what life would be like if we didn't have any specific expectations of outcome? You would simply be going along appreciating every new experience. There would be no judgment, no disappointment, no entitlement, no disenchantment, and no disillusionment. Without setting up expectations, you would be free to use your time in experiencing what is right before you. There would be no time wasted on projecting into the future and you would never feel short-changed.

What makes us feel disappointed and short-changed? When we have imagined how something should be and it just doesn't turn out to be that way— whether that is because someone else has dropped the ball, because we misinterpreted what was promised, or because we have created an image in our minds that doesn't match the reality.

The end result is that we feel somehow diminished by what actually occurs. But do we leave it alone? No! We compound the problem by going over and over it in our minds, and even confronting others that we choose to blame for not living up to our expectations.

Consider some of the ways that expectations rule our lives and see if any of these scenarios are yours:

- Our partners do not love us the way we think they should.

- Our bosses do not give us the credit we deserve.

- Our jobs do not provide for us the stimulation, challenge, and excitement we anticipated they would.

- Our vacations don't turn out to be as thrilling as we imagined they would be when we saw the brochure.

- Our neighbors are never friendly enough.

- Our children disappoint us by disregarding our advice and guidance, or not being attentive or grateful.

- Our heroes don't behave like heroes.

- Our houses don't retain the value that we believed they would when we bought them.

- Our retailers never have exactly what we want.

- Our partners aren't as successful as we want them to be.

- Our purchases don't fulfill what we expect them to do.

- Our teachers don't entertain us the way we want to be entertained in the classroom.

- Our parents have never respected and loved us the way we think we should be respected and loved.

Practical Conscious Creation Tip No. 20

Social-IZE Your Spiritual Growth

If you really want to hold yourself accountable for your spiritual growth, then share your affirmations and commitments with your social media community on Facebook or Twitter. Going public really puts your feet to the fire, but it also means that your Facebook friends and colleagues can be there to cheer you on and support you! Maybe you can even start a special social networking support group for your quest—sharing your experiences with others who are also on the same path!

- Our bodies don't maintain their health automatically without effort on our part.

These are just a sampling. I'm sure you can look at your life and see where your expectations are making you angry, frustrated, stuck, and unhappy—where your equilibrium has been destroyed by obsessing over what you think *should* happen.

Now let's back away from all of that and imagine what life would be like if you just let go of your expectations and set your equilibrium according to what is. By staying out of the future, and simply allowing life to unfold with wonder, enjoyment, amusement, and delight. Get rid of your measuring stick. Stop wasting time and emotional energy on creating expectations, evaluating what occurs, and fussing over things when they fall short.

You can create freedom and peace for yourself *by not assigning future value to what has yet to happen.* Let's take Dr. Browne's statement to heart: expectation is the death of serenity. Eliminate expectation, and serenity can indeed be yours!

Receiving: The Lost Art

There is much written in spiritual/self-help/motivational books about how important it is to give, but there is much less written about how vital it is to open yourself to receive.

In our modern culture, it is the strong male energy that is dominant. This male energy is proactive, aggressive, and out-reaching. Yet, spiritual teachers have known for eons that it is the feminine energy that is receptive, willing, and open.

Men in our world have difficulty with receiving. Most believe they must achieve, acquire, or conquer to gain. They don't feel comfortable when they receive—and especially from women—because they perceive that it diminishes their power. How often do you see men casually brush away gifts, praise, or acknowledgement? Few are masters of receiving with grace.

Many women today have assumed the mantle of masculine energy due to the demands of today's working environment. Their feminine energy is sublimated because of the need to fight to have all of their financial and material needs met. As a result, many women have also lost the ability to attract and receive passively.

So it is an art that men and women must relearn as we grow spiritually. Whether it is receiving money from new and unexpected sources, receiving assistance or help, receiving wisdom and guidance, receiving love and kindness, receiving praise and acknowledgement, receiving gifts, receiving honor, receiving peace and tranquility, receiving ease, or receiving unforeseen and wonderful opportunities—we must discover ways to make ourselves better vessels for receiving.

Here are some ways to cultivate the Art of Receiving:

- Commit more time to "being" than "doing." Stop and relax, be quiet and meditative. When you are active, you're not in the actively receptive mode. Slow down. Make sure you have enough rest.

- Ensure that the left side of your body (the feminine side) is unconstricted. Get massages, stretch, and use essential oils to make sure your left side has a free flow of energy.

- Consciously invite The Universe to send you gifts by intentioning: "I am willing to receive today." "I am open to receiving."

- When you are given anything—including praise—show your gratitude. Do not demur in embarrassment or brush it off. If you are not grateful for what you do receive, why should the Universe send you more?

- Whether you are a man or woman, indulge your feminine side. Pamper yourself using whatever tools bring you enjoyment. Men: Glory in the feel of silk shirts, or enjoy an occasional professional shave, for example. Women: Try wearing more feminine clothes, especially flowing and indulgent apparel; take bubble baths; or schedule spa days.

- Listen to soft music that puts you in a receptive, graceful, and contented mood.

- Visualize beautiful, rainbow-colored energy flowing to you from all different directions and filling your cells with brilliant radiance.

- Be in a vibration of love. Love is the most powerful attractor in the Universe, and it creates the signal that you are a deserving recipient.

- If you ask for something and it manifests, do not take it for granted. Feel the wonder of how effectively the Universe works. Wonder opens the door for more.

Practical Conscious Creation Tip No. 21

Thirty Days Without "I Can't"

Recently my physical trainer gave me an ultimatum: only one "I can't" during a session. The second one earns me extra repetitions! When you are lifting weights and you are fatigued, you really have to think twice about uttering that "C" word. By nature, people are self-limiting. We seem never to have enough faith or lack of fear to push beyond the point that we envision for ourselves. As my trainer has shown me, I can do more than I think I can if I just do it slowly and carefully, increasing a bit each time. So I challenge you to go 30 days without saying "I can't." And set a consequence for each time you do. I guarantee this will make you think twice about limiting yourself and it will open up new horizons and new self-confidence. Most of all, it will make you a more positive high-frequency person!

- Make sure there is fun in your life. If you are about all work and no play, there is no space for the new blessings to plant themselves. Have fun. Enjoy. Laughter and joy will open the door for you to receive more blessings.

- Say "yes." When the Universe puts something in your path, it may be a gift and you may not know why. Unless you are convinced that it is absolutely and clearly not in your highest good, say "yes" and see what gifts come forth. If you shut down too many opportunities, fewer will come.

- Be willing. Be aware. Be receptive. Be grateful.

May you receive in abundance, joy, and radiance!

What Makes You Suffer?

For most of humanity, the permanent state is suffering. I'm not speaking of physical suffering, but mental suffering.

What is it that makes us suffer? Thoughts that judge us, judge others, or that project our fears into the future.

Monitor for a day all thoughts that create anxiety or pain. You will be surprised at how much of your mental energy goes toward creating unnecessary suffering. Just think how much happiness you could have if you weren't worrying about things that have yet to occur, feeling insufficient in some way, feeling slighted or wronged by others, or being disappointed in other people?

It is the mental chatter that we create in our heads that gives us the most pain. Not our compassion for other people, not the external world. It is what is in our heads. These unfettered and out-of-control mental gymnastics are called variously: mental chatter, mind noise, the Monkey Mind, or "thought streaming" as termed by author Dr. Steve Pashko in his book, *Free Your Mind.*

So the key is to discover what leads to our mental suffering and learn to shut it down, or learn to "antidote" it. When you feel such suffering, you are not living in the present. You are somewhere in the past, in the future, or just generally elsewhere in your head, but you are not in the here and now and experiencing fully what is present and before you.

I recommend the following excellent books on the subject of alleviating mental suffering: *Loving What Is* by Byron Katie, *The Secret of Letting Go* by

Guy Finley, *Free Your Mind* by Steven Pashko, Ph.D., and *Quiet Your Mind* by John Selby.

In her book, *Loving What Is*, Katie advocates a simple and easy process that she calls "The Work." She counsels readers to run all repetitive, negative thoughts through the following filter:

- Is it true?

- Can you absolutely know that it's true?

- How do you react, what happens, when you believe that thought?

- Who would you be without the thought?

Once you spot thoughts of unnecessary suffering, you have the choice to simply shut them down, refute them, or do "The Work." This is an excellent process to begin managing one's negative mind chatter, but there are others.

Let's look at some of the thoughts that may make you suffer and the "antidote" for them:

- I am not *(pick one)*: "smart enough, thin enough, attractive enough, charming enough, gifted enough, as good as (insert name), and so on. . ."

  o **Antidote:** Learn to love yourself. There are numerous books and guides on how to increase your own self-love and acceptance. This is essential for your growth. However, until you do, use the mantra: "I am a blessing to myself, to this planet, and to all who know me." Replace all such ideas of unworthiness with this phrase. Dismiss any thoughts of "not enough" by repeating the phrase each time one of those negative impressions arises.

- I can never please *(pick one)*: "my spouse, my lover, my mother, my father, my siblings, my boss, and so on."

  o **Antidote:** You're living to make other people happy. Choose to be the best you can be and fully accept who you are. Be proud of your accomplishments. If you can do better, then do it, but don't judge yourself. And make your opinion the only one that counts.

- You believe someone has slighted or wronged you.

  o **Antidote:** It usually takes two to tango. You have to accept and feel wronged in order for that to happen. People can't DO to you; you have to let *them* DO to you. Choose not to feel wronged or slighted. *Move on!* Even if they have done something grievous, you have learned from the experience. See where you might have contributed to it, and if you determine you did not, then look for the message in the experience. Lastly, consider what you might have been doing to attract this experience and change it so you attract something different in the future.

- You are worried about *(whatever it is that could happen in the future)*.

    o **Antidote:** Stay in the moment, and simply ask yourself:

    — Is this true right now?

    — Am I "consciously" creating a negative future by dwelling on the unpleasant consequences of what *may* happen.

    — Can I influence my future by making a choice now?

    If you have acted on all your options, than let it go. Continue to bring your attention back to the present each time it drifts to the future.

- You are haunted by your past. You feel *(pick one)*: (guilt, shame, embarrassment, loss, disappointment, despair, fear).

    o **Antidote:** Here are some ways to deal with the thoughts and emotions of the past:

    — "Lance" them like a boil—which means bringing up the experience and allowing the festering emotions to air themselves out in the light of your reality today, to relive them with compassion and to reexamine them with the intention of releasing them.

    — Say "so-long" to them with love and gratitude: "Thank you for helping to keep me safe till now, but you no longer serve me. I'm directing you to complete your service. I will no longer require it."

    — Consciously say to yourself: "That is then, and this is now. I will no longer be a slave to my past."

    — Simply let memories and thoughts of the past slide by, as if they were a movie and do not engage with them. . . Don't dwell. Don't indulge. Don't get caught up in them. Let them fade out.

- You are creating false expectations, fantasies in your mind of what should happen and are then disappointed when they don't.

o **Antidote:** Stop projecting your expectations into the future, then you won't be disappointed. You will either be pleased with whatever unfolds or you will have the opportunity to act further. Either way you will have eliminated the headache of 1) worry/anxiety, and 2) disappointment with whatever doesn't match your fantasy.

- You feel like a victim (powerless, filled with self-pity, blaming others).

    o **Antidote:** Begin taking responsibility for your own life. No one can make you a victim. Once you embrace your power of Conscious Creation and begin creating your own life though personal frequency management, visualization and action, your thoughts and feelings of powerlessness will be a thing of the past.

- You feel envy, jealousy.

    o **Antidote:** Envy and jealousy stem from low self-esteem. Stop looking at other people's lives and start looking at your own. What can you do to grow and feel more confident and self-loving? What actions can you take in your life to feel more empowered and successful? What path can you create for yourself that is fulfilling? What are your personal goals, not via comparison of others? When you begin to act on these, then your thoughts of envy and jealousy will disappear.

- You feel stymied, frustrated, stuck.

    o **Antidote:** It may be that you are unclear or conflicted about where you want to head, or that fear (projecting into the future) is standing between you and where you want to go. Look to see where you may be unconsciously creating roadblocks and what you must do to gain clarity about your path. Take actions toward forward movement. Then let go of your thoughts of frustration. Stop dwelling. Just allow things to unfold.

Above all, when you are in the suffering mode, ask yourself:

- What's the truth here, right now?
- Am I living in the present?
- Is there an action I can take immediately?

Then release yourself from your prison, and begin living life unfettered.

Practical Conscious Creation Tip No. 22

Procrastination

Procrastination is a double whammy that can make marginally unpleasant tasks monstrous—and then drop your frequency into the dungeon, making you feel like there is a big weight on your head. So here's the key: Don't just do tasks *on time*; do them *ahead of time*! It's amazing what this act does to alleviate all kinds of stress. Knowing that your task is completed or "in the can" for the future elevates your frequency in a major way. One of my favorite things is to wrap up a project ahead of deadline and then go out and enjoy life because there's one less thing to think about. So as vacation approaches or the last days of summer when you can be laying by the pool or at the beach with your friends and family, don't ruin the experience feeling pressured to get a project done that could have been completed well before. . . Work forward and don't look back!

Oneness: How Do You Get There from Here?

The underlying and prevailing tenet of the spiritual movement is that we are all one small speck in an infinite unified matrix of the Universe. Each of us is thus an interactive part of this giant "force field" of energy that some would consider God or Source. Our energy is co-mingled and interchangeable with all other parts. Essentially, we are aspects of the great ONENESS of all things.

This fact has far-reaching ramifications—the most important of which is that every other human being is a component of oneself. Every animal, insect, or tree is a different reflection of ourselves. Earth is more than a place to live; it's our co-creative partner. If everyone accepted and acknowledged this, our world would be very different.

Today, our planet is dominated by the perception of separateness and competition. We view others as different or alien from us, Instead of embracing others with love, we perceive them with fear, suspicion, mistrust, and disregard. Instead of protecting many of the other life forms on this planet, we exploit them or eradicate them. We shamelessly misuse and destroy our natural resources, and the glorious gifts that Earth bestows on us. But we also diminish or abuse ourselves, forgetting what a precious spark of Universal Spirit—God or Goddess—that we are!

So what can each of us do to support, revere, and grow the awareness of this Oneness? How can we make our world better by acting from Oneness instead of Separateness? Here are some suggestions:

1. **Manage encounters with strangers and people who vex you differently.** When you meet new people, or when you are facing people who try your patience, take a deep breath and remember that they are part of you, an extension and reflection of your life force. This changes the complexion of the situation and reminds you that compassion, kindness, and a little more understanding can create a positive dynamic—one that opens the door for more love, kindness, and patience. Remembering you are both one, try to view the issue from the other person's eyes.

2. **Review your subtle prejudices and judgments:** Do you hold stereotypes about anyone? It could be related to their sex, income, neighborhood, ethnicity, job, homelessness, anything. People generally assume that prejudice

is mostly based on race, but the truth is that we often judge people and stereotype them for all kinds of other reasons. Look closely at this because you must remember to accept every individual for his/her uniqueness, and to embrace that person for his/her Universal Oneness.

3. **Stop competing!** Competition is about separation and a feeling of lacking something. Cooperation and collaboration is about Oneness. Consider your business practices or your striving for recognition when working in a group. How can you reach out to others in leadership, but also humbleness—without ego—to create greater synergy and benefit for all?

4. **Do what you can to support the planet and its inhabitants.** Watch your water and energy use, and reduce where you can. Don't be wasteful. Recycle. Share. Clean up after others who are not as aware or conscientious. Look after animals and the plant life. We are the caretakers of our brethren on Earth.

5. **Be loving, kind, and compassionate with yourself.** Before eating that big tub of ice cream, remember how important and precious you are to the Universe! As one very important expression of the Universe's wisdom and creativity, respect and love your body, your mind, and your spirit. Love and accept all aspects of yourself that reach for the highest good, and seek to gently change those aspects that are self-destructive or inhibiting. You are part of the Oneness, and therefore a treasured being. Love yourself as the Universe loves you, nurture yourself, and treat yourself with reverence for the infinite spirit that you are.

6. **Spread the Oneness:** Join others who share your views and find ways to educate the unenlightened. Volunteer to work with people who can benefit from receiving the message of Oneness to help change their perspective about life, about their community, and about themselves.

7. **Be in greater connection with the Universe:** Meditate, ask for guidance, and be open to receive whatever the Universe is seeking to provide to you—information, resources, support, and so on. Raise your frequency, and watch for the ways that you are being aided, guided, directed, and redirected by the Universe. As you open this channel of communication wider, you will feel your Oneness much more powerfully and with greater immediacy. You will truly begin to realize the blessings of your co-creational power with the Universe—blessings that are a direct result of the Oneness.

Practical Conscious Creation Tip No. 23

Bouncing Back

Are you a handball, a basketball, or a beach ball? When life knocks you down, can you bounce back like any of these? When you "take a hit," think of yourself as your favorite type of rubber ball and will yourself to bounce back! Smile when you think of yourself bouncing around like something in a Wiley Coyote cartoon! You have the strength and the resiliency! Happy bouncing!

Practical Conscious Creation Tip No. 24

Hold Out for Something Better

When you're faced with an option that you don't believe is in your highest good, don't take it because it seems to be your only option. *Believe* that there *is* something better on the horizon and hold out for that something better.

Chapter 3

Trust and Expansion

One of the most challenging tasks that we all face as humans is forward movement in the face of change, risk or fear. When we resist, we experience contraction, but when we are courageous, willing and trusting in our future success, we experience expansion. Expansion brings prosperity, abundance, peace, growth and beauty. So go forth and expand, living life with vitality and wonder!

The Gift of Risk

We face risk in almost every daily decision we make. Unfortunately, this is why many people are stuck in neutral in their lives—they are risk-averse.

How do you define risk? It is evaluating a new opportunity in light of standing steadfastly on previous ground. Risk is taking a leap into the unknown when you can safely stay where all the factors are known and familiar. What must a person give up to gain anew?

What most people do not realize, though, is that risk is really a gift. It is an opportunity to rise to a new level, to have and demonstrate courage, to sharpen our decision-making skills, to explore new vistas with eyes open, to gain self-confidence when we have chosen well, to force ourselves to confront limiting beliefs, and to discover and acknowledge our true capabilities. In other words, risk is an exceptional tool of spiritual growth.

Yes, risk can be scary, but it can also be a doorway to vast new personal and financial blessings. Accepting the right risks can mean new fortune, new love, new freedom, new expression, new joy, and more.

On the other hand there is a risk in not taking the risk. If you never say yes to taking your future in your own hands because you fear not having a paycheck, what might you lose? If you don't ask her to marry you because you fear commitment or constraint, what then happens when she accepts another proposal?

So how do we know which risks to take and which to forego?

1. **When the Calculated Risk Adds Up:** You have thoroughly evaluated the upside and downside versus what you would be sacrificing or changing. If your potential upside outweighs all else, take the risk.

2. **When The Only Thing Holding You Back is Fear:** If the opportunity has great promise and you're waffling because of "what if. . . " and you're envisioning all the scary reasons that things could go wrong, then turn it around and ask: "What if I didn't have any fear about this, would I do it?" Once you eliminate all the "made-up" scenarios, look at the reality, and if the opportunity is still strong, then do it! Fear should not be the reason holding you back from advancing.

3. **When You Have the Capital to Invest:** If you have enough to invest safely—whether that is your time, money, expertise, or emotional

capacity—then why not? Leverage what you have for something potentially greater.

4. **When It's Time to Burn the Ships:** If you have refused to move forward because it's safe where you are or you always want to have an "out," it's time to burn the ships. Without risk, there is no reward. Life can be very debilitating when you're in a rut. Take the risk and get out of the rut.

5. **When Where You're Going Could Be Better Than Where You've Been:** Sometimes you just have to take a risk because it can't get any worse than where you are. Risk in this case represents movement and progress because you're not really making a sacrifice. You can only go up from here.

6. **When Your Intuition, Instinct, or Internal Voice Urges You Onward:** Ah! A very important reason to say yes to the risk. Your divine connection is telling you there is a purpose for your soul in moving forward. Listen carefully in your quiet state, and hear what messages you are being given. Contrarily, if your inner voice tells you not to advance, do not ignore it. Wait till the next opportunity comes along.

7. **When It Feels Right:** There is a telltale sign that often indicates when you are on the right path. It simply "feels" right. You have a sense of expansion and openness. Project yourself ahead into the opportunity and see how you feel—is it expansive or is it constrictive? This should help guide your decision as to whether to take the risk.

8. **When Your Passion is Engaged:** If you are excited about the opportunity because it involves something you love, or it springboards you creatively, then clearly the Universe is going to help support you in the new endeavor. It is no guarantee of success, of course, because other factors may be at play, but your passion and love will energetically go a long way toward aligning the forces for success.

9. **When All the Synchronicities are Lining Up in Your Favor:** This is guidance that is leading you to make the change that this risk represents. If the Universe is already showing its support, isn't it time you climbed aboard?

10. **Consciously Create the Opportunity with Vision and Love:** Put your efforts toward using your extraordinary powers of Conscious Creation to manifest the success of the venture or decision, and minimize any of the risk. See it succeeding with no roadblocks, obstacles, or downsides. Then step into that new reality.

Making Decisions: Paralysis or Possibility

Nothing scares or paralyzes people more than having to make a decision! Why? Because people:

1) Are afraid of the unknown

2) Fear losing control

3) Think a decision is permanent and uncorrectable

4) Are afraid of and resistant to change

To avoid making a decision, people will allow whatever situation they are currently in to create pain, decline further, stop forward progress, or fester and infect everything else—none of which is healthy. Making a choice opens whole new vistas and allows you to rise above what no longer serves you.

Does this require great courage? Sometimes. It clearly requires a degree of courage. Does it require trust? Yes! Trust that moving forward is better than standing still, losing ground, or living with the guilt of watching forces overtake you. Trust that you can be successful by going forward with a clear vision, without fear, with flexibility and a willingness to learn from the experience—no matter how it turns out.

Flexibility is a very important element! First, once you make a decision, it may only be temporary. It may lead to new doors, or perhaps back where you came, with new information and new direction. Remember there is nothing more permanent in our world than change. If you are not unyielding and unbending, you should be able to make whatever adaptations are required to create value from the decision you have made. By knowing that every decision allows you new creative options and that you have the tools to be flexible and creative, you can release resistance and fear. You are not breaching a wall with no going back . . . you are being presented a new gateway to pass through. A new world to explore!

So let's look at some of the guideposts you can use in decision making. Employing these will give you more confidence about how to proceed.

Motivational speaker and author James Arthur Ray offers this useful procedure in his book, *Harmonic Wealth*:

If you are unsure when to move forward, ask yourself these four questions:

- Do I feel totally prepared?

- Is this decision/action in alignment with my vision?

- Will making this decision accelerate the achievement of my intention/vision/goal?

- If money were no issue, would I make this decision?

I'd like to offer you an additional series of questions to ask yourself if you are experiencing hesitation over a decision—regardless of whether this is for a business or personal matter. These include:

- **Are you clear on your vision?**

    o   Do you need to do more work on this? Have you a plan built from this vision that is strong, logical, and has a reasonable likelihood of success? What exactly is the desired outcome?

- **What preparation or homework would make you feel more capable of undertaking this decision?**

    o   Having the information you need and feeling prepared will increase your ability to make smart decisions based on real first-hand knowledge. It will give you more confidence in making the decision.

- **What are the possible extreme outcomes?**

    o   What's the worst-case scenario if it fails? Usually it's never really as bad as your irrational fears. It's possible you could just be back where you were before. So why not go forward? What's the possible upside? Look at both the moderate gain and then the wildly impossible gain if you truly have all the elements lined up in your favor? Look at what the amazing possibilities could be!

- **What's the upside versus the calculated risk?**

    o   Weigh the odds, as noted in the previous section. Review the upside and downside versus what you would be sacrificing or changing? Which side is the weightiest?

- **What does your intuition say?**

    o   Once you get that pesky fear out of the way, what does your intuition tell you? Get quiet and ask yourself. Ask for guidance and wisdom. How does your gut feel?

- **Does it incite your passion, do the possibilities excite you?**

    o   Do you feel surging energy and a sense of joy when you con-template the prospect? Or are you doing it because you think you should?

- **What do people you trust think about it?**

    o   Ultimately this is your decision. But it never hurts to hear what other people you trust (i.e. a mentor, a close friend, someone with experience in the field) have to say. Get feedback from one or two people who operate from a positive—and not a negative/fear-based—framework.

- **What is in your highest good, not someone else's?**

    o   Make sure this decision reflects what you think and what meets your needs—not from the viewpoint of what others think of you now or will think of you if you make this decision.

- **What if you were an objective observer?**

    o   Take away the emotional charge and look at it as if you were someone else. Would you still make this decision if it were not in-vested with a truckload of emotions?

- **Does this make good common sense or does the option represent un-realistic, wishful thinking?**

    o   While I fully support dreaming, visualizing, and engaging in the impossible, there must be a basis for reality in any decision. I don't want to discourage someone from making a great leap of faith, but certain decisions should take into consideration the facts as they are (i.e. you can't grow an orange from an apple tree). Base your decisions on good common sense—*plus* a sense of optimism and faith!

- **What would be your first action steps? Does that feel right?**

    o   Think it through beyond the initial decisions. What would you do next? How might you proceed? Then check to see how that *feels* to you. If you project yourself into the future, does this "feel" positive and uplifting?

Practical Conscious Creation Tip No. 25

Adaptibility

How often do you get "out of sorts" when things don't go exactly as planned? One of the nice aspects of becoming more spiritually aware and tuned-in is that you begin to "go with the flow," instead of getting "bent out of shape" when things are different from what you imagined or intended. Just try being adaptable the next time something goes awry! Consciously Create a state of peace and acceptance regarding the development. It obviously was meant to happen the way it did!

- **What resources (time, money, intellectual capital, emotional capital) can you truly afford to commit to it?**

  o What do you have now? What can you give that would still leave you with some base of support? Yes, sometimes you have to jump into the unknown, but if you can maintain a solid footing, it helps make a transition easier.

- **Can you move forward in increments rather than all at once?**

  o Not every decision has to be "all or nothing." Sometimes you can do it in increments, and as you gain one foothold, you can move to the next rung on the ladder.

It is always wonderful when you are decisive and know almost instantly you've made the right decision, but more often than not, making a decision is a process that proves its "rightness" through an evolution and validation. One must stay open to look for the reinforcement rather than be in a critical or judgmental mindset that looks for why it was the wrong move. Make your decision and allow it to be the first of many doors to freedom, joy, prosperity, peace, and love.

Taking That Leap of Faith

So how do you undertake that first step? How do you take that leap of faith when you are still scared and unsure at first? Here are some ways to ease into it!

1) **Breathe.** Take a deep breath. Breathe out the stale, complacent energy and breathe in fresh new energy. Do this 10 times and feel yourself relax into it.

2) **Meditate.** Get quiet and then get clear on where you are headed. Know what it is you want to achieve through this change. Take all of your fear, imagine bundling it up in a leak-proof container and shipping it to the center of the earth, where it is consumed in molten lava. Then open yourself to the support that the Universe is sending you. Bask in that gracious assistance and let it fill you with optimism and joy.

3) **Find your center—ground and empower yourself.** When you finish meditating, stand up, feet wide apart and solidly planted. Ground yourself by

seeing your feet as roots extending into the earth. Feel rooted and stable, gaining strength and steadfastness. Notice how you are starting to feel empowered. You have support from the Universe, you have stability from the earth. Now feel your own empowerment growing, filling your entire body. Observe this empowerment increasing in your heart! Experience this vibrant energy coursing through your system, and extending out through your aura or energy body. You are bursting with positive empowered energy.

4) **Declare your faith.** State your faith that the Universe will help guide you toward your highest good as you take this next all-important step. Know that the Universe is carrying you along in its embrace, welcoming your commitment. Express your gratitude for this assistance and for the doors that are opening to ease you into your new life.

5) **Discover your courage.** Like the Lion in the Wizard of Oz, uncover your hidden well of courage and let it flow. You are a courageous person; you were born with the ability to stand in your truth. Remember that you are not alone on the journey. You have help!

6) **Set your intention.** Now that you are clear about your ultimate goal or objective, state your intention to the Universe clearly and succinctly, in visual detail, and support it with the beautiful emotions of joy and wonder. Then write it, post it around your home, put it on a Vision Board or in a Vision Box. Do whatever you need to do to create it as a physical living embodiment of your intention for success.

7) **Act as if. . . Believe.** Even if you are having doubts about the outcome of your new endeavor, *act as if* it were to be a great success, and proceed vigorously, assuming that it will. Put your belief in the next step, then do it again with the one after.

8) **Let go of the how.** Don't worry about all the details. Sure, you need to plan, prepare, and activate the right steps to create a successful endeavor, but you don't have to know every detail ahead. You've set the course; the Universe will take care of the rest. Be open to "course correction" by the Universe, so you can take advantage of each new opportunity.

9) **Ask for guidance.** Just before you take your leap of faith, invite the Universe to direct you, counsel you, and create a smooth pathway. Remember that you must be open to receive this. If "receiving" is not easy for you, here is where you must adjust your "antenna," so that you don't deflect the wisdom coming your way.

Practical Conscious Creation Tip No. 26

Cancel!

As you grow spiritually, do you speak and then realize that you said something very counter to your new spiritual beliefs—something that just might manifest an unpleasant or unwanted experience? Does this happen when you are *even thinking* things that could manifest unhappily for you? Well don't despair. . . Many highly advanced spiritual beings (and some far less advanced!) use a very simple phrase to undo the damage. They say—or think—this word: Cancel! And then restate their desire or their thought in a more positive framework. It tells the Universe that you're taking responsibility and to disregard the errant statement or phrase—Please Universe, listen to the next one and act on that instead!

10) **Take the step—now's the time!** Quit that job, start a business, release an old relationship that doesn't serve you! Sell the old house and buy a new one, commit to an exercise program, move across the country, make a large investment in your self-growth, get married to the person you love—whatever it is, if you truly feel in your heart that this is something you passionately desire, then make the commitment and allow your glorious future to unfold before you!

The Power of Commitment

The Universe rewards commitment. Once you make a commitment, all the doors will open in your favor—in sequence! You may not know exactly how you're going to get where you plan to go, but once you make the commitment, you will be guided to the next step. And then the next. And the next one after that.

It's like that scene in just about every Indiana Jones or jungle adventure you've seen in the movies. The hero arrives at the chasm with no means across, and some wizened character says, "Trust. Just take the first step." And sure enough, a hanging bridge appears just as the hero's foot steps forward and with each step, more of the bridge appears.

That's the power of commitment. I'll bet that if you look back on your life, you can see this universal law in action. When you were passionate about something and you made the commitment to move forward, all of a sudden the doors started to fly open, people you needed showed up, synchronicities appeared, everything just fell into place.

So what commitment are you avoiding? Is it a big one or a little one? Does it involve habit change, career change, financial investment, home change, relationship change, releasing a co-dependent person from your life, addressing an addiction, or avoiding confronting a health challenge, for example?

So here's a good exercise to start getting comfortable with the idea of commitment. Write your commitment at the top of a page of paper. Then make a list of pros and cons. Make sure to add to the list of cons those statements that sum up the negatives of how you are really feeling, such as: "I'm unhappy. I'm afraid. I can live with what I'm making, even though it's poorly paying and I hate my job. I don't feel well, but if I have the operation, I could be worse."

Practical Conscious Creation Tip No. 27

Power of Suggestion

Hope you're not nodding off while you read this, but I wanted to remind you of the power of suggestion just before going to bed! There are three really good reasons for declaring what you want, for creating a vision just after you've put on your jammies and hopped into the sack. One is that you are allowing the power of your own subconscious to work on your wishes while you sleep. Second, you engage the power of the Universe to align with your wish (provided that it is riding your high-frequency energy.) Third, if you indeed believe in angels and guides, giving them your intention allows "your team" to work on it overnight and begin manifesting on your behalf. I can't tell you how many times I've gone to sleep desiring something to happen, only to find the answer, solution, or opportunity awaiting me in the morning. Now I go to sleep after giving my guides their assignment for the night! I find it really fun. Sometimes, I simply ask them to help me grow in certain ways and I don't always see the immediate results, but I know that they are there, guiding me toward my vision of what I want to become. I just find it easier and comforting to know I have help!

Then on the pros, write the upside: "I am so happy. I feel free. I have more money. My kids are benefiting because I feel radiant and can give them more of my time. I'm loving life. I have a great new home that I love. I'm living addiction-free. I don't have to worry any more now that I've had the operation. . ." You get the picture.

Most of us focus on the negatives, the risks, but hopefully this exercise will remind you of the extraordinary upside. And how could you fail when the whole Universe is lining up to help you once you make the commitment!

So stop waffling! Engage the power of commitment to create your dream and free yourself to move forward!

Just remember, however, that once you reach the next level, you will likely again find yourself at a crossroads. You can fall back to fear, or commit and trust again, because you know the exhilaration of succeeding through commitment. Take that first step!

It's a Universal Redirect!

Tired of making or encountering mistakes? What about hitting the wall? How about running into Murphy's Law? You make plans and God laughs? Then there are "problems," "challenges," "issues," "dead-ends," "failures," "disasters," "disappointments," "hiccups". . . I can go on and on.

But now hear this! These obstacles are not what you think they are. Forget those old labels. What you are experiencing are "Universal Redirects!"

How many times have you obsessed over what went wrong, perhaps blaming others or yourself? How often do you keep trying to work through something that isn't working? How much time have you wasted pushing a rock up a hill? How long have you hung onto problem clients or miserable relationships?

These are all symptoms that you have not yet realized that the Universe is offering you valuable information. Try something different! Change your attitude. Change your actions. Change your expectations. Change your team. Change your route. Change your job. Change your intention. Change your partner. Let go of this course of action!

Many people ignore the gentle nudges that the Universe offers until they

Practical Conscious Creation Tip No. 28

Going with the Change That Allows in the New

Recently, one of the leading quantum feng shui experts in the world offered to consult on my home. She spent an entire day here, and of course, knowing that her advice not only comes from thousands of years of ancient knowledge, but her own intuitive guidance, I am certainly following the recommendations she provided. But don't think this has been easy. It involved making many changes that meant letting go of the way things had been in my home—a home I'd lovingly put together. I've lived here for 15 years and was happy as it was. But making these changes allows for something new and exciting to come into my life. So instead of putting up resistance as I might have in the past, I trusted that this was the Universe's way of telling me that I had to open up space for something new, that this process would get me "unstuck" where energy wasn't moving. I feel blessed to have had this expert as a catalyst in helping me create and accept change to allow for something better to come in.

What can you change, shift or eliminate in your life to allow in something new—and maybe even better?

get hit with a sledgehammer. But all along the way, they're being redirected to new, more life-enhancing choices. Now here's the catch: If you don't do it, the Universe will do it for you!

I experienced this about 12 years ago when I was running my $2 million bicoastal public relations agency. It had become a burden—the fun had gone out of it. Instead of doing creative PR for my clients, I was chasing money to pay my enormous overhead. And furthermore, my heart was elsewhere, loving a hobby business that I had created selling mineral spheres. I saw the signs but just kept trying to juggle clients, vendors, and employees—with challenges everywhere. The business was imploding on itself, and I couldn't cut the cord. Finally, three clients all went into Chapter 11 bankruptcy in the same month, owing me $150,000! That was a very big ouch, and it was the last straw. I finally closed up the business, found another opportunity for myself immediately, and ultimately relaxed into enjoying life again after finding a way to settle with my creditors. The Universe was redirecting me to something far more life-enhancing than that stressful meat grinder I had suffered through those last two years.

When you hit a roadblock, instead of railing against fate, ask yourself: "What is this Universal Redirect all about? How can I look at this objectively, step aside, and think differently?" You've heard the phrase, "Everything happens for a reason." Apply that to your Universal Redirects and you will begin to see that each one is a blessing in disguise. There are no mistakes, no errors, no accidents, no missteps, no faults…There are only Universal Redirects!

Use these wonderful nudges as your guide early on, and you will find your life being easier and more effortless. Tune into the universal language of course correction and you will be rewarded with greater and quicker success, more peace and joy, less struggle, and greater abundance.

Just remember, if it's too hard, you're being called for a Universal Redirect!

Ten Ways to Learn to Trust the Universe

One of the questions I am most asked is, "How do I release my need to control and learn to trust the Universe?"

There is magic in trust and faith, as a growing number of books, articles, and videos devoted to the law of attraction and other spiritual laws underscore.

Increasingly, people are beginning to trust that the Universe has their highest good at heart, and this knowledge offers a path to greater peace, happiness, and prosperity.

My more than 30 years as a scholarship student and entrepreneur had convinced me that I needed to control every aspect of my life to ensure success. Yet, while I was successful, it never came easy—I worked very hard for my achievements and income.

Today, as a student of Conscious Creation and Universal Law—and someone who is much more open to the gift of divine teachings—I know that my successes come far easier if I allow things to unfold in divine timing, and live in the knowledge that my needs and desires are being met. My vibrational frequency is higher, and I am enjoying greater peace of mind.

Here's a perfect example of trust. This year, my resources have been committed to launching a new business, and I have not had the additional funds to take a vacation. So I simply asked the Universe if it could present me with a free vacation. Then I put the thought out of my head, knowing the Universe was at work on it. A few months later, I received a lovely invitation from a girlfriend who has built a new home with her husband in the Bahamas. I cashed in some airline miles and spent a beautiful week in Freeport!

As Napoleon Hill says in *Think and Grow Rich*: "Faith is the 'eternal elixir' which gives life, power and action to the impulse of thought." This idea can also be found in Ellen Peterson's book, *Choosing Joy, Creating Abundance*, where she states: "The truth is that your needs are met when you believe that they will be sufficiently met."

So here are some hints about how to grow your trust and confidence as I did over the past few years:

1. **Surrender and detach.** Let go of control, and allow the Universe to do its work. Create and visualize the end goal, then release it to the Universe and detach. Allow things to unfold.

2. **Look for little miracles.** By noticing and delighting in little miracles along the path toward your ultimate goal, you are reminded that the Universe is indeed working on your behalf. Look for little signs, small steps, and synchronicities. It's reinforcement for your trust.

3. **Watch as your needs are being fulfilled.** As your goals are achieved, you will gain confidence in the process of trusting the Universe. This will lead

to greater faith. You may even want to keep a journal of all that manifests. When you look back, you'll be surprised how many dreams came true over the course of a year!

4. **Remember it's all in divine timing.** If you get frustrated by the slowness with which your desires are being fulfilled, you resonate distrust. So back up. Remember that it is not your timing at work here; it's divine timing. The Universe knows better when to grant your wish than you do.

5. **Let go of resistance.** Don't push, don't react, don't force. Let it be. If you keep resisting or pushing back, you are not allowing the Universe to give you its grace easily and effortlessly. You are constricting the flow. It's another sign of mistrust. So just remind yourself to go with the flow.

6. **Tune into your higher self.** It's your ego that wants it now and is convinced your desire can't materialize without your manipulation and control. Turn it over to your higher self, your "heart self," and let it open the channel of trust with the Universe.

7. **God may have a better answer than you do.** Have confidence in the Universe to come up with the right solution. If you try to push through or mandate to the Universe the solution you believe is the correct one, you may be limiting yourself. If you postulate in your head how things should happen, you are narrowing the Universe's possibilities.

8. **Give up your problems—turn them over.** If you have a specific challenge that is confronting you, ask the Universe to take it from your shoulders and resolve it. Trust that it is then being handled and wait for answers.

9. **Believe the best.** Believe the best of people, circumstances and solutions. If you fret about all the ways things could go wrong, you again demonstrate your mistrust in the Universe. Assume that all will be well and when you turn it over, an elegant solution will turn up or that people will do their best.

10. **Listen deeply and follow guidance.** The Universe's answer to a challenge or the achievement of your goal may not be some external resolution. It may be guidance you are given, things you are directed to do or signs that you need to follow. Once you turn it over to the Universe with trust, listen deeply for the wisdom you are offered and follow the guidance.

Practical Conscious Creation Tip No. 29

It's Easier Than I Think!

Someone I know just gave me this wonderful piece of advice: If you are at all intimidated by something ahead, or worried about it being difficult or problematic, say this to yourself consistently: *It's easier than I think!* Stay in this thought and energy as you embark on the project and you may indeed find that *it is easier than you think!*

God Has My Back

I recently read a wonderful quote by singer Natalie Cole in a magazine. She said: "I know that God has had my back, even when I was screwing up."

How profound! What a simple, comforting thought: *"God has my back!"*

Even for people who have trouble with the concept of trust and surrender, thinking "God has my back" is a very simple and elegant way to realize that you are not alone and that you have an amazing support system already in place that you can rely on. It's a great way to realize that even in the worst of circumstances, God's hand is guiding you out of the morass and pointing you toward the light.

Just think about the times when you might have experienced this support system at work:

- When you were guided away from an ultimately dangerous or risky situation
- When money showed up at a time you needed it most
- When someone came to you with just the helping hand or the information you required
- When you got a "feeling" or "heard a voice in your head" that moved you toward or away from some action that ultimately turned out to be for your benefit
- When you were miraculously healed or were directed to a doctor, healer, or practitioner who helped you heal
- When a new client or new job showed up at the perfect time in the perfect way
- When you met your lover or partner through the most unlikely means
- When you were "in the right place at the right time"
- When you surely looked like you were headed for disaster and suddenly escaped

Even when I make a grievous mistake or am unkind or do self-destructive things, God still has my back. And even if I am slapped with the consequences of my bad behavior, that's still God looking out for me, teaching me that I must be more thoughtful, conscious, and compassionate.

What a relief! I am not alone and I have a powerful protector! Whether you are a dynamic leader who feels like everything must fall to you and you are alone on the precipice, or someone who feels weak and battered by life—with God at your back you can relax! When you relax, you become more intuitive, more confident, less pressured to make decisions that could be ill considered. Your frequency rises. You manifest more effectively. Your life is easier.

Just imagine going through life feeling that God is always there to nudge you in the right direction or pick you up when you fall. How would that change the way you feel about your life? Would it make life easier, more comfortable, less harrowing, more encouraging, more hopeful, less strenuous, less taxing, more forgiving? What would change in your attitude if you were always aware that God has your back?

Whether we know it or feel it, each of us deserves salvation in our lives—and by that I mean deliverance from unhappiness and unpleasant experiences. Sometimes we can be the architect of our salvation; other times we just need a little help. If God has your back, then you know that salvation is possible. That you can find a way. Or that you will be guided on the path—out of misery and pain.

And you know what? If you know in your heart that you have this great protection, then you can call upon it. Whether that is through prayer, meditation, Conscious Creation, or other ways—you can reach out to the divine Universal source and speed up your rescue by asking for assistance.

So don't forget God always has your back! You can take that to the bank!

Chapter 4

Conscious Living

Living Consciously is a way of life. The paramount principle of consciousness is being acutely aware of your responsibility for your actions, deeds and thoughts. You are cognizant of how your words and acts impact others and you are thoughtful and compassionate in how you express yourself. You are also careful to live your life as an example to others, and your values reflect your integrity. As a conscious being, you seek to live in harmony with the planet and all of its inhabitants. And most importantly, you recognize that you are connected to a spiritual essence that inspires you, cares for you, protects you and provides for your growth. In living a conscious lifestyle, you are honoring yourself and your creator.

Morning Rituals

Morning is rebirth, renewal, and reignition! It is a beautiful time to engage your connection with the Divine, set your intentions for the day, and step fully into your empowerment as a heart-centered light-being on the planet.

Each morning you can leave behind what was, who did what to you in the past, and how you did things previously. It's a new day!

But we can slip backward if we don't deliberately and consciously create separation from the past. Morning Rituals are a wonderful way to create that divide. They remind us of our brilliant power for reinvention of ourselves—a power that is indeed supported by our supreme Source.

I use my morning ritual to make a deliberate connection to God each day, to establish my gratitude, to ground myself, to consciously choose to come from a place of love, to set my intentions for the day, and to infuse myself with the essence of spiritual light that I wish to manifest in myself.

You can create or build your morning rituals around whatever purposes you deem most empowering in your life. So here are some that you can mix and match to create the ideal morning ritual for you.

- **Ground yourself.** We may often find that we are too much in our heads or "have our heads in the clouds." This is especially true for people who exist more in their spiritual or intellectual world than the practical world. But even for those who are savvy at negotiating the "real world," it is important to first ground yourself each day. As described earlier, simply plant your feet shoulder-width apart and visualize roots descending from your feet into the earth. Another way of making a connection is to visualize a string of golden light descending from above, through your midline, and into the ground. As an alternative, you can also simply wrap your arms around a tree.

- **Open to Source, connect to Source:** Deliberately open the portal between you and Source, allowing energy, wisdom, and guidance to flow into you.

- **Set general intentions.** Each morning I set my intention to have a day filled with joy, love, and prosperity, and to be of service to others. I ask for ease and effortlessness in all things. I seek to act more from my heart than from my head. I set my intention to trust the Universe and listen to guidance. My newest intention is to find wonder and beauty everywhere. What intentions can you set for yourself?

I'll let Rita Roberts, my dear friend and colleague, share her morning rituals:

> *When I wake up in the morning, before my feet touch the floor I set my intentions and align myself with them. I say: 'Today is a great day, and everything I need is in my path.' I make a commitment to stay true to what's in my heart and follow those desires because this is the path that's lined with answers and provision. I pray that God opens my eyes to see the answers that He's already provided. I remind myself that I too will be an answer for someone today. I also remind myself that I am well-loved and provided for. I set an intention to give my best, appreciate myself, and see the best in others and to be of assistance to others. I am then poised for love, progress, and adventure at every turn. With all of this in mind, I set my feet on the floor beside my bed and take my first step of the day into purpose and provision.*

- **Set specific intensions for or consciously create your day.** Create, review, and construct specific intentions for that particularly day as recommended in the first chapter of this book. What would you like to see happen? With whom would you like to have peaceful, successful, and collaborative meetings? How will you care for your health? What will you see yourself accomplishing? How do you see your relationship unfolding? And so on.

- **Infuse spiritual light.** Select the type of light that you would like to infuse throughout your body for protection, for change, for enlightenment, for manifestation, or for personal growth. I use the following types of light daily: Golden light for empowering Source energy; a mix of sparkling silver and gold for manifestation; sparkling pink for love; sparkling peach for joy; yellow for wisdom; green for health; blue for calmness and serenity; purple for spirituality. There are a number of books on the market that provide guidance on the various energy and aura colors.

- **Express gratitude.** When you begin your day with an expression of gratitude, it helps clear out negativity and raises your frequency. You can write or recite lists of things for which you are grateful or just allow your heart to express what inspires it that day. I always begin my morning ritual with the following statement: "Thank you for the blessings of this beautiful day." And I often conclude by saying: "Thank you for all the blessings I have now and all that are yet to come."

- **Be love—flowing love.** It is always my desire to be more loving and compassionate, to continue to open my heart. If this is also your desire, then put yourself in a state of love when you do your ritual. Be love, see it flow from your heart throughout your body, or up from the ground through every pore or down from the heavens into your crown chakra. Then stay for a minute in that state before allowing your love to flow out into the world.

- **Clear chakras.** It can be pleasant to do a little energetic housecleaning to start the day. This means doing a short meditation to clear your chakras of all blockages and expunge the dark, unwanted energy that clogs up the free flow.

- **Meditate/use guided meditations.** Your morning ritual can include a period of meditation to create inner peace and to allow for guidance to come through. You can do this on your own or with a guided meditation on CD or iPod.

- **Travel to the Fifth Dimension.** Imagine you are in the Fifth Dimension, where everything is connected by a grid of light. See yourself as you wish to be. Then ask to be made aware of all those individuals who can assist you with whatever you may need that day. Imagine them lighting up on the grid. Once you have identified them, imagine them connecting to you with a beam of light, heart to heart.

- **Use affirmations.** Speak any affirmations that you have created for yourself that inspire you to become *what* you desire and *who* you desire to be.

- **Do yoga, tai chi, qi gong, or another slow-movement, spiritually strengthening exercise.** Many people like to add a physical component to the beginning of their day. General exercise is great, but intentional, slow-movement spiritual practices are very compatible with a daily morning ritual.

- **Ask questions.** Ask questions that can open guidance, wisdom, and opportunity for you. For example: "How can I experience love today? How can I serve? How can I have a day of grace-filled ease and effortlessness? How can I be in wonder?"

- **Burn candles or incense.** Sensory aids enhance the morning spiritual inspiration and anchor your intentions.

- **Listen to or dance to inspiring music.** You can either set the mood with music, or start your day with body movement set to music that inspires you and opens your soul to joy.

Practical Conscious Creation Tip No. 30

Sacred Sundays

After years of having to work Sundays to manage the work load on my desk, this past year I began a practice that I call my "Sacred Sundays." Undoubtedly, there was wisdom in the Biblical mandate to keep the seventh day for holiness and sacredness. And while I don't go to a house of worship, my home is a house of worship. On my Sundays, I do the following things: treat myself to sleeping in, enjoy the pleasure of reading the full Sunday paper, meditate and dialogue with the Divine, read books, and exercise in the sun on nice days. I use the day to recharge my energy and reboot my mind. I've stopped reading emails and allowing outside intrusions. It's my day for myself, to ease my inner mind, take time out from the turmoil of life and remind myself of the universal support I have around me. I know that many people have responsibilities that won't allow them to spend a full day in self-care and self-regeneration, but I do encourage you to try to find at least a half-day every week to pamper yourself and shut out your world cares. It makes you so much more ready to enter the new week with a calmness and peacefulness that establishes a positive vibration that ripples forward. It helps prevent burn-out, and makes you more centered, self-confident and aligned. And if you're like me, it makes you happier! So here's to Sacred Sundays!

- **Sing/chant.** Whether you sing in the shower, sing praises to God, chant Buddhist sutras, or just sing whatever is in your heart, lifting your voice in song is a wonderful way to enhance a morning ritual.

- **Journal or write lists.** Grab that pen and start writing. You can put your intentions in writing, pour out whatever is in your mind and heart, or write lists of affirmations. Writing is a way to deepen your connection with God and create alignment.

So go forth and create—or refine—your morning ritual so that it serves to manifest your highest soul purpose and greatest joy!

Clear Your Cache

You've probably had the experience where you access a Web page that you know has been updated or changed, but your browser is still showing the same old page. You seek out your computer expert to find out why, and he tells you the only way to see the revised page is to "clear your cache." This means you must clear out the retained or temporary pages held in the browser memory so your new pages can appear.

The Universe operates very much on the same principle. As spiritual beings, we are charged with releasing the old before the new can be seen, experienced, and enjoyed. Do you really want to get stuck in life looking at old pages and doing the same things over again, suffering the same fate? Do you want to live with what you have or clear the way for something more appealing or exciting? New energy fills an energy vacuum.

If you are going to "clear the cache" from your own life, you will need to look at many areas and see what you can expel in favor of leaving space for what shows up next. So let's take a look at some of the areas that should be up for review.

- **Your Belief System:** This is the most critical sticking point in your personal browser! With all those old pages playing in the background, you'll find yourself reliving your experiences again and again. Look closely at what beliefs keep you stuck where you are, clear them out, and consciously replace each of them with a positive belief that opens the door for joy, prosperity, success, generosity, wonder, beauty, peace, and love. Then you can truly fly!

- **Your Attachments:** When you hold fast to old attachments, it means that you are anchored in one place—the attachments have claimed you. Look at releasing attachments in general, and specifically those that no longer serve you. One way to do that is to first imagine what life would be like without that attachment. If it feels freer and happier in your imagination, then cut that attachment loose! You can do this either for an emotional attachment or for a physical one, where you give it away, sell it, or destroy it.

- **Your Relationships:** It is often difficult to clear out unhealthy or withered relationships, but you won't have the emotional and energetic bandwidth for new ones if you're still pouring your soul into relationships that don't allow you to prosper. Look at relationships in every aspect of your life to see what needs jettisoning—employees/ employers/ colleagues/ business partners/ clients, friends, family members, lovers, spouses, and so on. And while this may not always mean completely cutting off all contact, it does mean that you need to stop feeding these relationships with your energy. Spiritually "clear your cache" and move on.

- **Your Habits:** If you look closely, you will undoubtedly discover a number of significant habits that are constricting your life. These are like little straightjackets that give you no room to move beyond the habit or rut you've created. These habits might be physical (smoking, being a four-hour-a-night couch potato, and so on), emotional (eating when you feel depressed, stressing when your workload increases, and so on) or spiritual (mistrusting everyone, being unkind, ignoring inner guidance, and so on). Wherever you have patterned behaviors that do not allow you the freedom to be a whole, happy, or self-actualized individual, then you need to start the clearing process.

- **Your Attitudes Toward Yourself:** Self-esteem issues are signs of unnecessary judgments against yourself. This leads to actions and behaviors that reflect your feelings of unworthiness toward self. Oftentimes this manifests in failure to take care of your physical body, your emotional needs, your personal care, your home environment, and your spiritual well-being. Look closely at each of these areas, start wiping clean the slate and allow in new attitudes of compassion, care, and commitment.

- **Your Attitudes Toward Others:** Have you engaged in any of these actions or emotions in the past months—unkindness, anger, mistrust, envy, condescension, intolerance, disregard, disloyalty, betrayal, condemnation, gossip? If you have, then you have not come from a place of love and compassion. It's time to clear the cache, start over and begin consciously reaching for your love and compassion switch before you act out.

- **Your "Take It For Granteds":** Too often our senses are dulled by our familiarity with an experience, a thing or a person that we take for granted because of its ongoing presence in our lives. How unfortunate! Because we then miss the delight, the joy, the wonder, and the gratitude of looking at something familiar with new eyes—as if it was brand new! So apply your cache-clearing skills to the familiar and see once again the wonder and the beauty of it! See that rose in your garden as if it was the first one ever! Appreciate your child's desire to play catch as if it was the first time and not the third this week! Be grateful for having such a skillful hairdresser that makes your color so perfect that everyone thinks you're a natural redhead.

- **Your Work Files:** Now we begin to get into the physical changes you can make in your environment. The Universe abhors clutter, so in order to attract new possibilities you must start discarding what is no longer of use and straightening, organizing, filing, and labeling what you are keeping. So begin with your work files. Declutter your office, and make space for new opportunities that can offer greater prosperity.

- **Your Personal Files:** Tackle the disorganized and old personal files at home or create files to gain control over piles of confusing documentation. Label by content and, if desired, by year. This should apply to your financial documentation, your household records, the articles you wish to keep stored, your recipes, your personal identification, your documents and passports, your contracts, your mortgage docs, your warranties, your correspondence, and your legal matters. However, check with your accountant to see how long you should keep financial information—some say five years and others say seven. Get rid of anything old and keep shedding the older information each year. You may want to store some of this on your computer, but make sure you have a backed-up hard drive.

- **Your Drawers and Cupboards:** This is where clutter accumulates and you are not even aware of it until something falls out on your head or the drawer is so full you can't close it. Before it gets to that point, go through every drawer or cupboard in your house and start tossing old, useless items, including those items you can't figure out why you had in the first place! Rigorously attack food pantries, kitchen drawers, bedroom drawers, bathroom cabinets, and so on. Don't just toss; organize! Put like things together. For example, I have now reorganized all of my Band-aids into separate containers based on size and shape. As a result, I spend far less time sorting through them to find the one I want. You and the Universe will "breathe easier" once you've done this, and you'll have more time to spend on joyful activities instead of looking for things you want or need amidst the mess.

- **Home, Garage, and Attic:** Junk the junk! That's job one. Then start eliminating things that don't fit your life any longer—furniture you don't like but that once belonged to your grandparents, design features that are out of style, colors and objects that are no longer in keeping with where you are spiritually, items that take too much care, things that don't work and you fantasize you'll fix someday, pieces of your old life with ex-husbands and ex-wives, and so on. Think of it as "housecleaning for happiness."

- **Your Garden:** Your garden is a reflection of the state of your life. Let your neighbors and the Universe see a lovely space free of weeds, unkempt plants, overgrown trees, trash, old equipment and tools, children's toys, or anything that takes away from order, cleanliness, and beauty.

- **Your Clothes:** You have probably already been urged to clear out your old clothes from your closet for spiritual and space-making reasons. This is definitely an important "clear your cache" action. First, let go of all clothing you no longer like, then clothing that doesn't fit, then items that don't flatter you. Ask yourself honestly if you can still see yourself wearing each piece in the next year. If not, put it in the "to-go" pile. This includes shoes, belts, purses, and accessories. When done, organize the remainder by color and category. You'll save time if you always know where something is because it's where it belongs.

- **Your Old Medicines, Vitamins, and Exercise Equipment:** Don't clutter your medicine cabinets, counter tops, and home with out-outdated stuff you don't or can no longer use. If you bring in something new, commit to using it. Don't let it go to waste.

- **Your Old Books:** Most of us hold onto books just because we paid for them and received some educational or enjoyment value from them. But books can simply be an added drain on your space and your spiritual shelf if you just accumulate them. So go through and determine which ones really hold value for you today and which you can pass along to someone else who might appreciate them. You may find that you have outgrown your old collection of James Bond novels, or that your current spiritual values don't mesh with books from your days as a practicing Catholic, or that books about war don't reflect who you are today.

"Clear Your Cache" and open the way for new miracles!

Practical Conscious Creation Tip No. 31

Letting Go of Negative Energy Objects—
"Clear Your Cache" Bonus Tip

Take a walk around your home and let your energy tell you what no longer serves you. If you get a negative feeling about something, or you think: "Oh that's ugly and I'm only keeping it because my sister gave it to me," it's time for it to go! Give away anything that makes you feel unhappy, represents unpleasant memories, does not fit within the realm of being life enhancing or beautiful, or is no longer useful. Allow someone else to love it. Leave room in your home only for those objects that inspire you and support your high-frequency vibrations.

No Kvetching Allowed Here!

A couple of years ago, one of my close friends, a woman I mentored for many years, sent me a plaque for my kitchen wall that she knew I would appreciate. It reads: NO KVETCHING ALLOWED HERE! Kvetching is a wonderfully expressive Yiddish word (the Jewish cultural language) that means "complaining." Doesn't the word kvetch even sound like a whiney complaint?

You can be a kvetch (a complainer) or you can kvetch (the act of complaining or kvetching). Noun or verb, it doesn't matter which—it means you're an emotional drain on yourself and everyone else around you!

Complaining—or kvetching—is an habitual glass-half-empty approach to life. And complainers aren't content to stew in their own misery, unhappy with everything around them, and all the people they judge to fall short. They feel compelled to share it with the world! But does everyone else want to hear it? Not likely. I remember, when people would ask my grandfather how he was, he would say: "Fine! What's the use of complaining? No one wants to hear it anyway."

Whether a kvetch wants to build support to justify his or her point of view, needs to feel "heard," or wants to make someone else bend to their will, it's a dead-end tactic. The noisy wheel seldom really does get the grease. Whining and complaining usually achieves just the opposite tack, it stymies real change because people don't like or want to accommodate a person who is an unpleasant annoyance. As the saying goes: "You get more bees with honey than vinegar." It's a far better strategy than "being a noisy wheel."

And worse, that negative energy continues a pattern of unconsciously attracting more of what the kvetch doesn't want. Remember, where you place your focus is what you attract!

Most of us are not even aware of our own kvetching. We're just commenting on whatever we don't like. And we may even surround ourselves with other kvetches for comfort. Kvetches tend to reinforce each other's negative views on life.

But what if you made your sphere of influence—your home, your work, your social environment—a Kvetch-Free Zone? How might life change?

- You'll be happier, no longer weighed down by all those negative words and thoughts

- You'll raise your personal frequency and may begin manifesting increasingly positive experiences

- You'll have more upbeat, positive friends

- Your family and friends will notice a new lightness in you and may even follow suit

- People will more likely do what you recommend or suggest since you aren't being critical

- You'll become a more endearing and lovable person who creates light wherever you go!

How do you break yourself of the kvetching habit?

- When someone asks you how you are—tell them all the good things and skip the bad!

- Start a little daily journal and write down every complaint or negative comment that comes out of your mouth. (Oops, was that me! Did I say that?) This will be illuminating because you'll realize how much of your daily conversation is complaining!

- Punish yourself for every complaint. Put a dollar in a jar for charity or give another dollar tip to the next waiter or waitress that serves you.

- Make a pact with someone you love (a spouse, sibling, parent, close friend) to have them gently point out when you are complaining again.

- Note when other people are kvetching, but don't correct them and don't commiserate. It's your little wakeup call, making you aware that this is what you sound like.

- Post signs in your home that read NO KVETCHING ALLOWED HERE wherever you spend time talking to others—near the phone, on your computer, on your mirror where you start your day, in the kitchen when you are making dinner for your family, spouse or significant other. You can substitute the word "Whining" if you choose.

- Set an intention to stop complaining, and ask your guides and angels to tap you on the shoulder before you say something negative so that you can reframe your thought. You then have a choice to either say nothing at all or to say it differently.

Practical Conscious Creation Tip No. 32

Accountability Buddies

Sometimes an Accountability Buddy is what it takes to help you fulfill a commitment to yourself. For many years I have been challenged by the priority of putting my work before taking care of myself. This translates into starting exercise and weight loss programs, and not staying with them. Then I would feel guilty, berate myself, and just feel worse. "I know better, but why can't I stay with it?" These are not exactly high-frequency thoughts and emotions. But this year I was ready to make the commitment. The key, though, is that I didn't do it alone, where I could just slip back into old habits; I committed to a workout trainer three days a week. He also tracks my food via an online log, and on the days I don't see him, I ride my exercise bike. Guess what? It's now more than five months and I'm staying on track. The reason? I have someone to whom I must be accountable. I can't make excuses, I can't *not go* or I pay for the sessions. I work to please both him and myself with my progress. Sure there are a lot of days I don't feel like going, but I do and I feel better. Most of all, I can feel my self-respect and my self-love restoring. I'm releasing pounds slowly—more slowly than I'm used to—but I'm also not so manic and panicked. This is a process. Now I have someone to support me—and to whom I must report. So the message is, if you are having difficulty making a commitment to something in your life, try an Accountability Buddy—whether friend, master-mind partner, or professional. It could very well get you over the hurdle and into a new way of life that indeed raises your frequency!

I encourage you to break the habit of kvetching before it costs you friends, a job, clients, a relationship, or a peaceful, joyful, and prosperous life! Don't worry: You can become a *kveller* instead—someone who *kvells* speaks effusively about how wonderful things are!

Where is Your Sanctuary?

Life can be tough, especially when, for so many of us, finances are strained and job security is nonexistent. The pressures of ensuring a steady stream of income, holding onto a home, fulfilling family responsibilities, taking care of commitments, and just dealing with the pressures of daily living are oftentimes overwhelming.

Each of us can feel alone, harried, and frazzled. We feel resentful, angry, bitter, exhausted, moody, irritated, and lost. Our soul cries out for relief, for sanctuary!

Most of us cannot take the time or may not have the resources to run off to an ashram in India for two months like Elizabeth Gilbert did in *Eat, Pray, Love*. We have to find our own sanctuary closer to home. So where do you go to rest, recover, and connect to God and your higher self—the place where you can just breathe and feel safe? It could be:

- A quiet place in your home where no one will bother you, where you can meditate and just become peaceful

- A yoga, qi gong, or tai chi class

- Outside in nature—a special little area where you can sit, or a place you can walk, or in the garden, perhaps

- A house of worship or spiritual center

- By the ocean listening to the soothing waves. In the mountains surrounded by all the pines. In a meadow blooming with flowers

- A place that offers quiet meditative music

- A spiritual retreat guided by a spiritual leader, yogi, or other wise person

- With animals that lighten and delight your heart

- On the massage table

Practical Conscious Creation Tip No. 33

Air Out Your House

Our homes are often places of stuck energy. Throw open the doors and windows and air out your house. This isn't just about fresh air; it's about circulating the energy and releasing the negative vibrations that have been closed in. Borrow from the Native American tradition and burn a bit of sage to "smudge" as a means to further purify and cleanse the energy. Open up to new, clean, high-frequency vibrations!

- At a day spa

- In the bathtub, surrounded by candles and quiet music

- Inside you—wherever you are!

Create a regular place of sanctuary where you can go when life just gets overwhelming, or to simply destress before it gets that way. You can do this alone—or with a friend who shares your need for quiet relaxed communion with self, higher self, and the Universe. Mark certain days on the calendar just for self-sanctuary.

May you find peace, joy, and deliverance from anguish and stress in your place of self-sanctuary!

How Do You Handle Stress?

Stress. In today's world, this is not easy to avoid. Unless you are a yogi, Buddhist monk, or Hindu holy man, you probably are suffering the effects. Stress takes its toll on our health, our mental stability/resilience/acuity, our eating habits, our fitness, our sleep, our attitudes, our outlook, our patience, and our families and partners. Stress comes from financial concerns, jobs, home life, relationships, parental responsibilities, time limitations, and what we expect of ourselves.

How do you handle stress today? Do you complain to everyone around you, snap at people, suffer from insomnia, cope with stress-induced physical ailments, bury yourself in more work to avoid what's happening at home, sleep to escape, drink, do drugs, overeat or become depressed? Think about it. What behaviors do you have that are your response to stress? Make a list.

But here's the thing: *stress is all in our heads!* It's really not physical. There's no giant boulder sitting on our shoulders. Stress is completely manufactured in our minds. If we choose not to indulge in stress, it doesn't exist! I know people who just let everything roll off their backs. They go blithely through life, trusting that everything will turn out fine and choosing not to bother themselves over what other people say and do to pressure them. Most of these people are a lot happier than the average stressed-out person! And certainly spiritual monks, who have divested themselves of most worldly possessions, have often managed to find the path leading toward nirvana.

But if you are not quite as spiritually evolved as those euphoric individuals who have found ways to totally eliminate stress from their lives, there are ways to at least mitigate it in yours.

Let's look at constructive, spiritually enhancing methods to cope with, respond to, or prevent stress.

- **Ask the Universe to take some of the load.** Make a list of all the things for which you feel responsible or that you must do. Then carve out the biggest, more important ones for yourself. Put the rest on a separate list that you ask the Universe to begin handling for you. Then let go of your worry over those items.

- **Meditate or have "quiet time" every day.** Find a time of day when you can carve out 20 minutes and just go inside yourself, let go of everything else and say, "I am at peace." See radiant blue light flooding your body from above, and going into each cell. Blue is calming and peaceful. This little oasis should open up a more soothing spiritual space in your mind and your heart.

- **Exercise.** You probably already know this is great stress relief and good for your spiritual body as well. Try to make time at least three times a week.

- **Recover your sleep.** Ask yourself, "Is this really worth losing sleep over?" It probably isn't. First, set an intention to go to sleep and to release your concerns to the Universe. And if that doesn't work, try a bit of self-hypnosis. Count down from five, telling each part of your body to relax from the feet to your head. Then say, "As soon as I exit this hypnotic state, I am going deeply, easily, and quickly to sleep." Repeat this three times. Then count up to five, and close your eyes.

- **Curb self-destructive behavior.** Whenever you have an urge to do something addictive, sing! Or do something ridiculous that makes you laugh. Tell a joke. Take a happiness timeout. Smell a rose. Watch the squirrels climb the trees. Go for a short walk. Play with your puppy.

- **Don't deny yourself vacations and time off.** Make sure you take at least *two weeks* of vacation a year, even if it is scattered over long weekends. You must get a break from unrelieved pressure and responsibilities. Take your birthday off and go celebrate! This is spiritual survival!

- **Organize your life.** Life becomes more frantic and stressful when you can't find things easily, when your house is a mess, when your desk is a disaster

Practical Conscious Creation Tip No. 34
Who is On Your Team Beside God?

In life we either build teams or try to go it alone. It's a lot more fun and life is much easier if we progress forward in teams. We can also achieve more if we indeed have people at work who are "the wind beneath your wings." But our team members can also be family members or friends... anyone who helps to lighten our load by carrying some of the burden. I am so fortunate to have staff, mastermind partners, business partners, consultants and friends that I can call upon when I need them or who are already in place assisting me to do my work. I can't imagine how difficult it would be to do all of this without help—and I am so deeply grateful for their aid. So look around and see who is on your team. Write a list of what they do for you. Look to see where there are holes in your "batting lineup." Then figure out who else you can recruit to join your team—officially or unofficially! Team members can be workers, advisors, or people who provide emotional support and other kinds of assistance. Check to see who can carry more than they are now and be excited to take on new roles. Look at your family members, your roommate or your significant other and where they might be willing to provide more support. Do NOT go through life trying to do it all alone. That will only make you bitter, unhappy and overworked. So be a Conscious Creator and build your team around you with a vortex of joy and shared purpose. Gift your team with continual praise, recognition and gratitude and they will only grow in their support of you! (And don't forget to reciprocate when your team members need a hand...)

I call mine "Team Lapin"...what's yours?

area. Neatness lends itself to calmness. You can let go of the need for control because all is in order.

- **Find someone to give you comfort.** You don't have to be alone. Find someone with compassion who will listen and be sympathetic. That person may not have the answers, but just listening will make you feel better. You can be that person's Confession Buddy, too.

- **Be compassionate with yourself!** When you are being kind to yourself, it's easier to be kind to others. If you are being self-critical and putting pressure on yourself to live up to unreal expectations, you will likely treat others unkindly. If your superiors are pressuring you to perform, you might just take it out on your co-workers or your spouse. Recognize that you are doing the very best that you can and be happy with your contribution. Your company/boss/business doesn't own your soul. You are just loaning the company some of your workday hours. Give your very best during those hours.

- **Stop worrying!** Fretting never made anything better. If you have a sudden brainstorm that solves a problem or lifts a concern, act on it, offer it and move on. Don't obsess. Don't distress. Have confidence that you'll be guided to know the answer or have the solution when you need it. Or maybe it isn't even your problem to solve!

So in closing, imagine a beautiful domed shield of golden light around you and let the stress bounce right off. Your soul needs that buffer. You have a choice of whether to allow your ego to keep you in a stressed-out state, or let your heart put you in a blissed-out state. Which would you prefer?

Meditation for the Meditation-Challenged

So you've tried meditating, and you're not sure you're actually getting it right. You want to meditate for many reasons: you've learned that it is the best way to access your intuition, guidance, and universal wisdom; you've heard that meditating gives you a doorway to inner peace and tranquility; you're aware of the studies that reveal the medical benefits of meditation—lower blood pressure, increased sense of well-being, faster healing.

But meditating isn't that easy. You sit still for a long time, try to close out those thoughts speeding across your mind, all the while engaging in rhythmic deep breathing. . . Do you visualize your future? Do you listen for guidance? How is this supposed to work?

The answer is that finding the right meditation practice is like finding a therapist. You have to try a few different ones until you find one that works for you. So below I have assembled many different options from which you may choose. I encourage you to try a variety until you have a growing sense of comfort—and you don't have the annoying urge to just get it over with!

I'll begin with my personal favorites:

Sending and Receiving

As a Conscious Creator, you know that much of your power in creating your own reality is visualizing how you want your life to be. But if you have a limited time for meditation, say 30–40 minutes a day, how do you both deliver your intentions and clear your mind to receive guidance? My solution has been to do a sending-receiving meditation. The first half of my meditation is devoted to sending my desires to the Universe, visualizing with emotion whatever I wish to see manifested. The second half I commit to receiving, blanking my mind, putting out my "antenna," and allowing messages and guidance to come forth. I begin that second process by asking God/the Universe what it wants me to know that day, then stay open to whatever comes through.

Just Be

Oftentimes we think there is a right way and a wrong way to do something. But the blessing of meditation is that we don't have to do anything. We can just be. When you get quiet, simply eliminate any should or shouldn'ts. Release everything that binds you, worries you, or makes demands of you. Just let your soul be. It's a profound sense of relaxation to not have to do anything. Breath in, breath out. Just be. Be with yourself. Be with the oneness. Be with the source. Be at peace. Just be.

Breathing

There are many, many versions of meditative breathing, but most recommend that you breathe deeply from your abdomen. Inhale and exhale to a steady rhythm. Some suggest breathing in through your nose and out through your mouth. The point is to focus on your breath so it becomes almost hypnotic and takes you away from any outside stimulus.

Here are some options:

- Breathe one beat in and one beat out

- Two beats in to four slow beats out

- Count up to 10 breaths and then reverse the count down to one. Then repeat.

- Count to 100 and start over. Or count from 100 down.

Objective Observer

One way to release yourself from the tyranny of your thoughts is to make yourself an innocent bystander. As your thoughts float by, just notice them as if you were an observer and let them escape. Don't judge. Don't shoo them away. Just observe and refocus on your own inner place.

Mindfulness

Mindfulness is the practice of focusing exclusive on what is going on in or around you. You become totally focused on what you are feeling physically or emotionally to the exclusion of everything else. You notice how your buttocks feels as it is pressed to the ground, where it has contact, if your muscles are tensed or relaxed, if it feels cushioned or pressed onto a hard surface. You become aware of what each part of you is experiencing internally and externally. To perform mindfulness meditation, become aware of all your sensations. This forces you to stay present. "All that is asked is that you bring compassionate attention to what you are experiencing, moment by moment," says Dr. Jeffrey Brantley in his book, *Calming Your Anxious Mind*.

Here are some mindfulness meditations:

- Begin at the top of your head and slowly become mindful of your scalp and how it feels. Then deliberately take individual segments of your body and do the same, slowly moving down your frame until you reach the tips of your toes.

- Do this same mindfulness meditation while walking.

- Scan your body for emotional blocks or constrictions. Wherever your feel constricted, ask what it is about, then encourage your body to begin releasing the emotion. Scan again to see if it is now feeling more open. Do this until you can feel the energy flow cleanly everywhere.

- Breathe mindfully. Become aware of the breath coming in, going down your body, expanding your lungs, and pressing against your belly. Feel it come back up slowly and feel it rise up through your mouth.

- Sit quietly in nature and become aware of every sound, every color, every movement, every element—taking each one at a time. Allow yourself to feel you are part of this natural world.

Mantras and Chants

Spoken-word meditation is the ideal solution for some who have difficulty releasing or calming their thoughts. Focusing on a word or phrase repeatedly, coupled with rhythmic breathing creates the vibration that draws in and anchors spirit, or creates a peaceful space for your soul to express itself.

Try some of these:

- "I am" phrases. Pick one and repeat: I am love. I am joy. I am peace. I am a gift. I am healthy. I am beautiful. I am worthy. I am loved. I am lovable.

- Breathing in and out one single word—"peace" for instance.

- Repeating phrases of oneness: "I am that; that I am." "God and me." "God and I are One."

- Breathe in love and breathe out fear.

- Recommended by authors Peter Cole and Daisy Reese in their book, *True Self, True Wealth*: "I am always connected" (in-breath); "Spirit guides my path" (out-breath).

- Chanting the sacred Sanskrit mantra OM.

- Chanting various other mantras considered powerful aids in manifesting dreams and engendering enlightenment: The Sanskrit chant *Aum Namah Shivaya* or the traditional Buddhist chants *Nam Myoho Renge Kyo* or *Om Mani Padme Hum*

- Do these chants while fingering sacred strings of beads.

Eyes Open/Focused Meditations

Whereas many meditators prefer to keep their eyes closed and shut out the world, others enjoy a focused, eyes-open approach. One of the goals of such a practice is to join your essence with an item that holds your gaze. You will be merging and exchanging energy and creating the opening for spiritual inspiration.

Among those subjects favored by many are:

- A candle flame, which is the spark of life, purifying all things

- Flowers, which represent beauty and the female essence of the planet

- A picture or image of Buddha or Quan Yin, the goddess of compassion

- A crystal or sphere, which embodies certain properties for healing or growth

- Sacred designs that have special meaning to you, sacred geometry, or perhaps mandalas

- A card drawn from a "divination" deck, which points the way for your spiritual expansion

- A photograph of someone with traits you aspire to

Sound Meditation

Audio inspiration is a nice addition for meditators. While silence is golden, sound can be a doorway to heightened awareness and elevated states of consciousness. Some meditators also prefer to listen to guided meditations as a way to relax and bring themselves to a fully present meditative state.

Here are some of the options for sound meditation:

- **Singing Bowls:** The vibrational sounds of singing bowls are soul stirring and powerful.

- **Music:** New Age, healing, and spiritually inspirational music is the perfect accompaniment to meditation, taking you deeper into a peaceful state.

- **Sacred Chants:** Recorded chants from Buddhist and other enlightened cultures are powerful aids.

- **Drums:** Sounds of Native American, Asian, and other cultures' drumming circles can be a meditation aid for people who wish to lose themselves in the beat.

- **Recorded Meditations:** There is a wide variety of guided meditation CDs available on the market. Many are of a general relaxing nature, but others are designed to help facilitate growth or healing in a specific area of one's life.

- **Recordings to Change the Brain Rhythm and Consciousness Level:** A growing number of companies are offering special meditative CDs or downloads designed to change your brainwave pattern and take you deeper into altered states of consciousness. What might take an hour to do on your own, these products can do in a few minutes, especially if played regularly.

Visualization

As a Conscious Creator, you no doubt know the power of visualization for manifestation, but visual images can also be used for many meditative purposes and help open you to guidance, to purify, to imbue yourself with some desired trait or state of mind, or to just relax.

Here are some ways to practice visual meditation:

- **Sacred Scene:** Imagine yourself in some beautifully natural place or a golden temple in the presence of God, guides, and angels. Transport your mind and heart to a place of wisdom, grace, and love.

- **Chakra Clearing:** Imagine each chakra, the seven beautiful vortexes of energy along your center meridian in their individual radiant colors (red/root chakra/your place in the world; orange/second chakra/sexuality, money, creativity; yellow/third chakra/self-esteem and emotions; green/heart chakra/love; blue/throat chakra/speaking your truth; indigo/third-eye chakra/intuition; purple/crown chakra/your spiritual connection to Source). Carefully and intentionally clear each one of any blockages so that it can spin easily and efficiently to support your physical, emotional, and spiritual well-being.

- **Color:** See yourself swathed in colorful energy emanating from the Universe in a pyramid of light, saturating every cell of your body.

- **Love Meditation:** To increase the love in your life, create a meditation where you are surrounded by love in all ways in all places from all sources. See yourself receiving love. Then also imagine yourself flowing that love to others.

- **Meditation for Health:** To improve your health or address a specific health consideration, imagine a little candle flame or spark of vibrant energy illuminating each and every cell that needs healing. Imagine yourself fully healed in all ways, doing the things that your perfect health affords you.

So let me close with two thoughts about meditation. One of the blessings of meditating is that you are letting go of the past and the future, and you are letting in the truth of now in this one peaceful moment. The other is a reminder offered by author Caroline Reynolds in her book, *Spiritual Fitness*: "The important thing to remember is to meditate not with your mind, but with your heart."

Practical Conscious Creation Tip No. 35

Hypnosis

One the best ways to start reprogramming yourself to be in a higher vibration state—and to release limiting fears and anxieties—is to engage in self-hypnosis. You can read simple directions on self-hypnosis at *www.wikihow.com/ perform-self-hypnosis*. This relaxing practice enables you to bypass your conscious mind and your ego and to change your beliefs. Some people find it easy to perform self-hypnosis, while others prefer external stimulus or direction. There are wonderful guided meditations available to address many personal challenges and limiting beliefs. You'll find hypnosis-based downloads and CDs a great tool to start shifting your vibration.

Grieving With Grace

If you've suffered the loss of a loved one recently, my heart goes out to you at this painful time in your life. I know it feels as if the pain will never fade, but it will if you open your heart. Let me offer you some Conscious Creation thoughts to aid in the releasing process.

Allow yourself to go through this grieving period. It's okay. By releasing this emotion now, you will not harbor it deep inside your body where it can do damage and create illness in the future. Let it out. Grieve alone, but also be with others whom you love and who love you—people who remind you of the gift you are to the planet.

It is truly important to celebrate your loved one, not just mourn! I love the concept of an Irish wake where people get together, party, and tell great stories about the transitioned person. We threw a wonderful memorial for my mom, not a funeral. All her friends came and told a story about her and how she influenced their lives. Yes I cried, but I cried tears of a joy. It was a fitting tribute to my mother's life.

Focus not on being alone or about the negative aspects of your loved one's passing. Focus on the joy you are going to create for yourself, the joy he or she would want for you to have. Fill your life with things that make you feel good—a luxurious hot bath, a massage, going on a hike with a friend, picking cherries, photographing poppies, bringing flowers into your home, enjoying music, playing with a pet (and if you don't have one, now's the time to get one!). Do whatever makes you feel good. Your loved one would want that for you and so does the Universe.

Music is a great soothing power. Pick music that makes you feel good, whether that's quiet New Age music, classical, or even rock or pop. If you like to dance, then dance! If you are a *Grey's Anatomy* fan, you might recall Meredith and Christina "dancing out" their frustrations, pain, and anguish. Dancing is soul release.

When you must clear your loved one's things from the house, find others who can use and appreciate them. That will create great karma on many levels. If you can't face the dispensing yourself, call a charity in your community and have them come pick up the contents. We gave 5,000 romance novels to the battered women's shelter in our community when my mom passed. Just think of the fun that created for those women who never even knew her! She would have loved it!

Provided you have the time, one of the most healing things you can do is to serve others. It gets you out of your head and into the wonderful high vibration of giving. So find some group, organization, or cause that will allow you to give of yourself in positive and loving ways. This will bring goodness back into your life.

When you meditate, get centered and peaceful. Then bless your loved one's guidance and love for all these years. Put a smile on your face and remember one great memory. Then quiet your mind again and ask the Universe: "What shall I do next? What shall I *know* next?" Stay open to the message even if it doesn't come right then. I assure you that when you ask the Universe questions and you listen for the answers, you will receive amazing guidance and love. Remember that you are loved! Remember that you are embraced by the Universe and have support and direction at all times.

Allow yourself to soak up all the comfort from your friends, family, and co-workers. Sometimes we want to put on a strong front, but it's okay to be vulnerable and just receive the gracious gift of other people's attention. But remind them that it's a time to celebrate your loved one's life as well, thereby raising the vibration to a positive one. While it's okay to feel your sadness for now, you have the power to shift your sadness to a higher vibration that will serve you better as you leave your grief behind.

Your life continues. Make it a rewarding one, filled with joy, love, peace, and service. Envisage a good life, and you shall have it. That's the greatest gift you can give your loved one, to let that person know that he or she gave you the foundation to create a wonderful life anew.

Practical Conscious Creation Tip No. 36

Feeling Isolated?

If you are someone on the path of non-religious spiritual connection and personal growth, living within a community that tends toward conservative values and traditional religious practices, you may be feeling alone and isolated. To achieve a sense of belonging, you will need to reach out. One choice is to go online and participate in communities with like-minded people. However, another is to make a commitment at least once a month to attend and participate in some type of organization that unites the conscious community in your region. You can seek out a New Thought Spiritual Center (*www.newthought.org/members.html*); look for or start a "Meet Up" meeting (*www.meetup.com*), or participate in/volunteer for a nonprofit with conscious values (environment, wellness, animal welfare, aiding the under privileged, and so on). Get connected!

Chapter 5

Clarity

Clarity is critical. In Conscious Creation, if we are not certain of what we want to happen, if we are hobbled by beliefs that are inconsistent with our vision, or if we are simply unsure or confused by the choices confronting us, the Universe cannot deliver what we THINK we want. The Universe requires clarity for it to act. Put in an order, and then it can be delivered. Clear, strong, directed energy creates reality. Dither around with diffused energy, and the molecules cannot assemble into anything that resembles your desire.

No doubt you've often heard the success stories of people who have written specific descriptions of the loving partner they want to attract or the home they desire to have. There is little mystery in this process. It's a function of clarity. Get clear on what you want and you'll be one of the next success stories.

What Would My Soul Do?

Most of the time when we are faced with choices and decisions, we agonize over them because of all of the baggage we have built up over the years. Our decisions are made more difficult because of fears, anxieties, past memories, and other emotions that press in from all corners. We allow our mind-chatter, mistrust, and self-doubts to project all kinds of negative consequences and these either cause indecision, delayed decision, or the wrong decision. Even if we make the right decision, we have agonized over it and suffered the painful process of sorting through the baggage before we get to the relief of commitment. And even then, we may second-guess ourselves.

Imagine that you were your soul. Your soul is filled with light and joy! This incredible being vibrates with love and peace. It is completely trusting in the Universe to guide it, and has at hand the faith that every decision is one that will lead to its highest good. This soul has a knowingness, it taps into the Zero Point or Unified Field to gain information that allows it to make a good decision, and it relies on an intuition that is always right. The soul is a repository of integrity and honesty, making choices that show respect for its existence and honor for the other souls in which it comes in contact. This soul recognizes that we are all one and that there is no separation between beings, so it blesses each contact with another soul with love, kindness, and compassion. It sees in each and every other being that soul's dignity and demonstrates appreciation for the path it has taken.

Essentially, your soul is a clean slate that brings only its joy and love to the party. It doesn't have all the other baggage that your earthly human life has amassed. It is free of all restrictions, pain, anguish, and limitations. All it asks is, "Does this lead me to expansion, light, and love?"

So, as you go about your life, why not ask, "What would my soul do?" Just let go of all the other mind-chatter, pare back to basics, and ask this one simple question: "What would my free, expansive, happy spirit do in this circumstance?" Then, get quiet, go deep into yourself, and open the door for your soul to answer.

Unencumbered by all the worries, anxieties, and history, your soul can make a clear decision based on your highest good. With the freedom of not being weighed down, it can fly! It will soar with the knowledge of the right decision, guided by the Universe, embraced by God. Note how this feels to you in your

Practical Conscious Creation Tip No. 37

Divination/Life Choice Cards

What are Divination Cards or Life Choice Cards? These are themed decks of cards that help guide people in making decisions about their lives. Guided by your higher self, the premise is that you will select cards with key messages that resonate with your life at that moment. You can use them to simply learn more about your state of mind and heart by picking cards randomly, or you can ask specific questions before selecting your cards. It is astounding that whenever I select a card, it seems to be so perfectly attuned to what I need to know—whether that is a gentle lesson, a pat on the back for something accomplished, an encouragement, or a piece of truthful, but perhaps painful wisdom. I recommend using such cards to help you connect to the infinite store of wisdom, defining how it applies to you in your life at this particular moment.

emotional core! Clear, joyful, easy, peaceful, confident, relieved? That's what you should be feeling if your soul takes the lead.

Now you may still have to consider the consequences for others close to you when you make your decision, but at least you will have the wisdom of knowing what your spirit believes is right for you before you make your final commitment. And this clear knowledge and wisdom should be given the weightiest consideration. If you must compromise your soul's guidance to accommodate the circumstances, then at least use this wisdom as a compass to where you ultimately want to go. And begin Consciously Creating a good outcome for the decision to be made for an even better opportunity in the future to fully implement your soul's guidance.

"What would my soul do?" Whether this is about a relationship, a career move, a financial decision, a health matter, or anything else—this one question can simplify your life. It can allow all of the nonessentials that hold you back when you are faced with a situation to drop away, enabling you to see more clearly what is truly in your highest good, focusing on what is really important, being decisive, and blazing a trail to a happier, more productive, more relevant, and more soul-satisfying life.

What Would You Miss If You Died Today?

At some point in our lives, each of us looks back and realizes that another year has passed without achieving our most cherished dreams and desires.

Some people never act on their dreams. Some wait until they are too old to fulfill or enjoy them, and others just try to do it all in the last years of their lives. But why wait?

This topic became evident when I started to ask myself a very important question and realized how critical the answer is: What would I miss if I died today? What didn't I do? What didn't I do *enough* of? What gives me so much joy that I would be sorry if I left this planet without having experienced it or indulged myself further in it?

This is not just a matter of whether I bought a fancy convertible to go driving with the top down. It's also a matter of the experience I want to have in this life. For me, for instance, I would like to love more. I would also passionately enjoy traveling more and fulfilling my desire to do an online photo gallery of my travels. I would regret if I didn't do more of these things before I exit this physical world.

What would you miss if you died today? I recommend that you put some serious thought into this question, then create and execute a plan to live life more fully in the coming days, doing more of the things that come up for you in this self-examination process.

Here are some of the ways you can start down this road:

1. **Make a "Bucket List."** You don't have to wait till you nearly "kick the bucket" to do a *"Bucket List"* (like in the popular movie). Do it now! When you are still young and alive! List all the things you want to do, to experience, in which you yearn to immerse yourself. What would you miss if you hadn't done it or done more of it?

2. **Create a vision.** Set aside some meditation time to visualize yourself doing these things and experiencing them fully. Use your power of Conscious Creation—even if you currently don't have the money, the time, the knowledge, the opportunity, or the person with whom to share the expense. Start the energy flowing outward to attract back the means to experience the desired intention.

3. **Commit to doing at least one thing a month and mark your calendar.** One sure way to really start fully living your dream is to commit to doing one thing on your list every month. Mark it on your calendar. Make plans. Go online and sign up for what you need or what you want to do. You can do something different each month, or you can just continue to focus on one specific aspect. For instance, if your Bucket List includes creating artworks, going down to the tide pools with your kids, and creating more romance in your relationship, you could sign up for a painting class one month, take the kids to the tide pools the next, and plan a surprise romantic dinner with your spouse for the third month. Or you could simply focus on one of these—creating a romantic interlude on the same Saturday each month, for instance. You could delay the painting classes for a few months and do them toward the end of the year, once the romance has returned as a daily experience in your married life. And make sure to find time to take the kids to the tide pools in between!

4. **Do more of what you love.** For some people, it's really just a matter of making more time to do something that you already pursue. Let's say you

Practical Conscious Creation Tip No. 38

Who Can I Emulate?

While each of us can focus with intention on the traits we wish to develop in ourselves, some people find it easier to look at someone else and think, *That's how I want to be!* Whether that is a close friend, someone you see on the street, a person you watch on TV news, a celebrity who gives generously to causes, or a Mother Teresa, other people can be a touchstone. This is not to say that you should be jealous or envious, that you should wish to be them, or that you should worship them. It is only to say that people who exhibit worthy traits can be your inspiration to begin Consciously Creating those traits in yourself.

love to fish, but you only go once a year. Commit to at least four trips a year and plan them in advance, so you don't back out. Let's say you love to read historical romances, but you're just so busy you only average one a year. Create "reading days or weekends" in your calendar, so that you work with your commitments and your family to carve out special time for you to enjoy this guilty pleasure.

5. **Spend more time with the people you love.** Don't wait till you're at the end of your life or theirs to spend more time with the people you love— be they friends, relatives, or lovers. Don't pine for them and miss them! Go see them. Book your visits well in advance on your calendar, or do something spontaneous! Just act now!

6. **Tell someone you love them.** Don't forget to tell the people you love how much you love and appreciate them on a regular basis. Let your heart and your voice speak what you feel now so you don't have any regrets in the future.

7. **Heal a breach.** People tend to have the greatest regrets around not having healed the breach with relatives or other people they love. So make amends, forgive now, and get this off your Bucket List for good!

8. **Do one thing for someone to give them joy.** What would you like to do for someone else that they would not or could not do for themselves? Make sure you put one of these on your list, too, because surely there is some part of you that would miss this opportunity if you didn't do it in your life-time. Figure out what this would be and for whom and then act on it!

Practical Conscious Creation Tip No. 39

All Is Well

All is well. Wouldn't it be nice if we all operated from this premise instead of: "Oh No! What disaster is going to befall me next?" I recently attended an event and before each session, we were asked to put our hands over our hearts and say, "All is well." Whew! That felt soooo good! It just made me relax into a state of wonder, trust, and peace. I also have a charming Scottish yoga teacher, who always says in her sweet Scottish brogue, "Everything is good!" Such people remind us that the world really is perfect and that everything is happening just as it should— that our lives are unfolding in ways that are helping us to grow and evolve, and few things are ever as bad as we make them out to be in our heads. We assign negative value to them. So start tomorrow from the premise that *All is well* and greet the day with a smile! Then sit back and remember that phrase each time you hit a speed bump! You'll be surprised at the difference it'll make!

Chapter 6

Happiness and Peace

I have good news for you: You weren't put on this earth to be miserable! That's something I've been telling people for most of my life—something that I just knew innately. But as I was researching my book, *The Art of Conscious Creation: How You Can Transform the World*, my strongly held beliefs were reinforced.

Virtually every great spiritual leader on the planet says that we come here in a state of joy and then proceed to muck it up. Our souls are blissful things—looking to love, live deliciously, and enjoy. Furthermore, the Universe is programmed to give us all that we desire—to "download" to us goodwill, happiness, and peace.

So why do we persist in wallowing in misery and suffering? Because we can't believe our good fortune, and we question it, question and doubt ourselves, refuse to trust, allow our egos to get in the way of our good sense and spiritual knowledge, deny reality and truth, and ultimately let ourselves sink into negative thinking. Then our negative thinking and focus on "what's wrong with our lives" magnetically attracts everything that will reinforce our unhappiness.

Grab Life's Joystick

But I said there was good news at the beginning of this chapter. Want some more? We can choose not to be miserable. We can "grab life's joystick" and Consciously Create happiness and bliss in our lives!

So how does one grab life's joystick? Here are some ideas:

1. **Choose to be happy!** Think positive thoughts. When you feel a wave of negativity come over you, consciously rearrange the thought to something more optimistic and hopeful. When you do that, be confident that your words are creating a positive, happy outcome. Counter unhappy thoughts by taking a moment of joy. Put your mind into a lovely dream of bliss and allow those feelings to wash over you! My personal favorite is to be overrun with adorable, loving, cuddly puppies!

2. **Stop thinking less of yourself and think more of yourself.** Love yourself more. Pat yourself on the back more. Pamper yourself more. Give yourself a break. Focus on your strengths and not your failings. Enjoy who you are. Allow yourself to feel pride in whatever you have done and who you have become.

3. **Do something daring!** Whatever it is that you have denied yourself or been afraid to do—just go do it! Kick start your "aliveness" by fulfilling a dream and experiencing that rush!

4. **Release the shackles of the past.** What you did or experienced before has no bearing on what will happen tomorrow unless you bring it forward. You can alter patterns at will. Remember, today is all that counts. What can you do today to be happy and fill tomorrow with contentment? What choices can you make that are life-enhancing and not self-destructive?

5. **Make your own decisions.** Stop doing anything just because you think you *should* or that you believe is what others want of you. This is your life and no one else's. Do what you believe is right for *you*—and whatever it is that you desire to do.

6. **"This too shall pass."** When I feel oppressed by a problem, I simply remember this gift of wisdom passed down to me by my mother. Knowing that solutions always come in time, and that I will be freed of this issue sometime in the future, allows me to let go of it in the moment. Try it for yourself!

7. **Liberate yourself.** Stop fretting over things you can do nothing about, or over other people's issues. They are not yours to solve. Remember the wisdom of the Serenity Prayer:

    God grant me the serenity
    to accept the things I cannot change;
    the courage to change the things I can;
    and the wisdom to know the difference.

8. **Connect!** Oftentimes we feel alone and isolated by work schedules and commitments. Make time to talk to someone you love or who loves you on days when you need a lift. Reach out to a partner, a relative, a friend, a mentor, or a counselor to help bring you back to equilibrium. Be a good friend or supporter for someone else and see your own personal satisfaction rise.

9. **Wrap up a project.** Attend to something that needs fixing, finishing, or focus. Taking it off your "to do" list will elevate your spirit.

10. **Set a goal and attain it.** It is human nature to feel great when you have accomplished a task or achieved a milestone. Whether it's a small step (walking around the block each day) or a major one (climbing Mount Rainier), meet or exceed your own expectations and bask in the glory.

11. **Discover one of your gifts.** Try something new! Look for your hidden genius. Recognize a special ability that you can share with the world. Especially if you are feeling unworthy. Search for whatever skills you have that bring out your natural talents.

12. **Do one wonderful thing every day.** Treat yourself to a favorite book or ice cream cone. Exercise until you feel the endorphins let loose! Go hiking with friends. Take your dog to the park. Read to your children. Play your

flute. Make a bouquet from your garden flowers. You get the picture.

13. **Enjoy your own company.** Let go of the soul-crushing need to always be doing something just for the sake of not being alone, to be with a lover or friend, or have the TV on in the background. You don't need to be with someone to validate your worth. It's wonderful to reach the point when you can be alone and happy. Discover how special you are. Go to the movies on your own. Meditate and be peaceful. Take yourself out for a nice dinner. Enjoy your spiritual practices. Indulge in some creative hobby. Journal your thoughts. Appreciate whatever is going on around you. Just discover the pleasure of you!

14. **Go out and help somebody else.** Nothing makes us feel better about life than that wonderful emotion we experience when we've given our time and effort to help someone and their gratitude washes over us. Be nice to everyone. Put a smile on your face, and be the sunshine that lights up the room. Compliment a person who toils daily without much acknowledgement.

15. **Start a Bliss Blog.** Let your followers know what is contributing to the happiness in your life. Illuminate for them how you find joy in each day, and therefore be an inspiration for others to find their bliss.

16. **Hang with happy people.** Surround yourself with people who are naturally happy or who know how to look on the bright side. Don't be jealous of their good nature. Learn from them and join with them.

17. **Spend a little time every day Consciously Creating fun and joy.** Make a list of everything delightful you would like to come your way. Cut out pictures from magazines and put these in a special box, with words on the cover that say: "Thank you for granting these wonderful things to me." Then trust that the Universe is working on bringing them to you.

18. **Get out in nature.** Feel the wonder that comes from being outdoors, from sitting in the sun, walking on the beach, smelling flowers, resting under a tree, enjoying the brisk wind, or playing at the park. The mere act of soaking up nature's positive energy should raise your own energy and personal outlook.

19. **Count your blessings!**

These are just a few ways that you can start living a joyful and happy life. But it takes a commitment to begin Consciously Creating your own happiness.

You have to take responsibility for your own bliss. You must not look to anyone or anything to manifest it for you, clear the obstacles, or magically make your life perfect. You are the only one who can open the door and invite that joy into your life. So go "grab life's joystick!"

Shifting from Disappointment

As the economy contracted, nearly everyone was touched by disappointment in some way—whether it was the loss of a home, loss of a job, loss of freedom, loss of security, loss of peace of mind, loss of a dream, or loss of someone you loved who could not cope.

We each go into our lives having high hopes for love, abundance, and joy, and many times we can indeed experience those for long periods of time. But what's really difficult for most of us is to reach a certain level of success and then see it slip away. That's what has been so debilitating for many people in these past few years. And whether it has been because of our own poor choices of mortgaging our future on credit cards and houses that we cannot truly afford, or whether we have done everything right and watched our 401K investment disappear—it is heart-wrenching to deal with the sense of loss.

But wallowing in the disappointment only creates a negative energy vortex that continues the downward spiral. If you must, allow yourself a short period of time to grieve for what was. This is actually a good step in processing the emotions. But do not stay there and do not allow this to fester into anger, resentment, envy, or bitterness.

You must begin shifting away from disappointment, so you can begin co-creating either a recovery to better times or a new vision of what your life can be. Let go of what was. Whatever is ahead will be different—maybe even better. Accepting that change is inevitable is the first step to creating a shift, rather than resenting change or holding to the past.

Now what positive goal can you focus upon? What vision can you create that will help to readjust your attitude and your vibration? What vibration can you begin emitting that will be a match for where you want to head?

Chose a specific emotion or thought to consciously vibrate. Is it love? Is it joy? Is it fun? Is it beauty? Is it gratitude? Is it the enrichment of nature? Is it a closer connection to Source? When you are in disappointment, you want to keep it simple. Give yourself uncomplicated and simple goals. Choose one of these. Get up each day thinking about this. Take breaks during the day to focus on it. Check in at dinner time. Breathe it in. Just breathe. Go to sleep holding these thoughts and dreams.

Be on Negative Energy Watch. Wear a rubber band and snap it when you have a negative thought or reflect on your disappointment from the recent past. Laugh at yourself and then get up and get a glass of water. Wash your negative energy down with a long slow drink. See your new positive energy filling up your tank.

Spend time with positive people. If you find yourself with other folks who are bemoaning their lives, either encourage a change by suggesting everyone shift their attention to something better, or change the company you keep.

Do activities that bring laughter and fun. These don't have to be costly. Ride bikes, roller-skate, go to or rent movies, sing, dance, exercise, play board games, play poker with fun-loving people (for chips, not money!), read uplifting books or romances, call a friend long distance using free weekend minutes, go visit someone you love and haven't seen in a long time who lives in a nearby town, plot your future conquests of the heart, play with children you adore, take your dog on a hike, or watch your kitty with a ball of yarn.

Just remember *believing* that you will experience what you choose to envision is a key component for allowing it to happen. So truly believe that great days are coming!

Now, if that disappointment flutters back in, shoo it away with a litany of gratitude. Maybe your portfolio is down and you're scraping to pay medical bills, but your daughter is about to graduate college, you have the most amazing touch with decorating on a budget, the neighbors are letting you take all the plums off their trees that you could possibly want, your boyfriend has happily rediscovered his talent on the guitar and serenades you. . .

You get the idea. Life is not money. Life is life. Find what is good about it and create more of it by appreciating what you do have. See the silver lining and not the grey cloud.

Vibrate away the disappointment. Vibrate the joy and abundance that you are already—and that you live on a daily basis. More will come. *Shift happens.*

Practical Conscious Creation Tip No. 40

Remember: It's Only Clouds

I recently began meditating on a rainy day and asked the Universe what I should know that day. The answer was quite profound, and I want to share it with you. I was reminded that despite there being rain clouds "gloomying" up the day, the sun was actually shining and it was a beautiful day. I just couldn't see that because I allowed the dark rain clouds to occlude my vision and my mood. What I was being told is that our minds are the same as the clouds. Life is really beautiful, and perfect. We just let the negative thoughts and chatter in our heads cloudy up our vision and our attitude. So just ignore the clouds and remember the sunshine. Whenever the chatter gets loud in your head and you think about being miserable, recall it's beautiful just on the other side. You are actually basking in sun if you just keep that in mind! The sun is still shining, and life is good! Just let it be good!

Ten Ways to Celebrate Yourself and Your Achievements

When was the last time you patted yourself on the back? I know, we are always told that it's not polite to laud yourself, that you should be humble. But there's a problem with that philosophy: It conveniently lets you overlook your own contributions to the world and reinforces the idea that your value is insignificant.

Nothing could be farther from the truth! *Everything* you do is significant—to yourself, to others around you, and to the world at large. And when you perform acts or tasks that are particularly outstanding, important, inspired, creative, kind, or expansive beyond your previous expertise or experience, you deserve to be recognized. Whether that recognition is from outside yourself or simply inside, it is imperative to acknowledge your success and growth.

If you are like me, you often rush through your day looking ahead at the tasks on your "to do" list or the things you must accomplish by the end of the week. You are focused on the future, and you have skipped over what you might just have done. I have been very fortunate to have been in a coaching program with the elegant visionary personal growth leader Barbara De Angelis, who reminded me that I seldom stop and applaud myself for all of the things I accomplish. I'm always thinking about what's next. In so doing, I minimize what I *have* achieved.

This is focusing on *lack*. I look at my book sales and think, "What am I not doing, where have I not marketed my book?" instead of, "Look how far we've come in sales and how many people we are influencing to change their lives!" Or I think "I'm not reaching enough people to deliver my message of Conscious Creation," instead of saying, "Wow, now I have a fantastic video on the website of myself speaking to an audience, I have a speech I love, a PowerPoint presentation, a speaker's packet, a flyer promoting my speaking engagements, and I'm poised to do more professional speaking!"

Do you do this, too—minimize your achievements while you narrow your focus to what you haven't yet done?

If we want to raise our personal frequency, there's no better way than recognizing our own personal achievements, relaxing into our success, and feeling good about what we've accomplished before setting off on the next quest!

So we have to stop, breathe, and pat ourselves on the back. This is abundance in action. This is compassion for ourselves and gratitude for our own gifts.

You must shift how you look at your own life and mine it for the myriad successes you forget to celebrate. To consciously own your own wonderful achievements, start a list of 10 achievements you should celebrate. Done that? Okay. Now make a list of 10 ways to celebrate those achievements!

To create your list of achievements, look at everything you do in your life. Don't minimize simple tasks that you take for granted, but I encourage you to pick the achievements that have been the greatest stretch for you—those that required effort, intellect, creativity, perseverance, love, or inspiration. Then periodically make sure that you stop and practice self-appreciation with one of the following 10 celebrations—or others you might create:

1. Give yourself a minimum of 15 minutes of reverent silence and gleeful pride! (It's okay to be proud as long as you are not gloating over others!)

2. Share with your dearest friends, your lover, or your family your joy over your victories and achievements. They will assuredly mirror back wonderful happiness and encouragement for you. Of course, thank them for their support.

3. Write a letter to yourself extolling your achievements, your talents, and your special abilities that enabled you to be successful. Be grateful to yourself, as well as the Universe!

4. Light a candle and bask in its flame. Light incense and drink in the scent of your success. Enjoy the sunset with a nice glass of wine.

5. Take a long luxurious bubble bath and think about what you've achieved. (Alternatively, jump in the Jacuzzi or spa and indulge yourself with a long soak.)

6. Spend part of the day outdoors in nature renewing your appreciation for yourself, reinforced and blessed by the flowers, the animals, and the positive energy of the sun.

7. Take a day off, and once an hour remember why you've earned that day.

8. Make or go out for a nice dinner and invite someone you want to celebrate with.

9. Get a massage or go to the day spa, so you can treat your body and your mind with pampering love!

10. Keep a journal of your achievements and look it over weekly, monthly, and again on New Year's Eve Day. Toast your achievements at year's end, along with some special friends. Toast theirs, too!

So here's a toast to you! Pause and recognize how wonderful and unique you are—and what a gift you are to this world!

Practical Conscious Creation Tip No. 41

The Best is Yet to Come!

Most people spend their lives looking backward at their fondest experiences and worrying that life is getting away from them. That's a good way to fritter away the rest of your life without living it. If you want to make sure that life is just one great experience after another, hold the vision that "The best is yet to come!" And believe it!

Chapter 7

Love and Compassion

Do you want a happier, easier life? Then surf the love vibration! Is life a bit of a struggle? Do you find yourself thwarted at work, unhappy at home, yearning for romance, feeling unappreciated? Then love is your answer. Not romantic love, but universal love—the kind that opens the doors of infinite possibilities.

Consider for example the last time you had a disagreement with a co-worker. Did you show your anger or disappointment? What happened? Did you create tension? Did you get your way? What was the cost? What about the last fight you had with your lover or spouse? Could your negative approach have made things worse? If you do see yourself in these descriptions, then maybe you are ready to try Surfing the Love Vibration.

Surf The Love Vibration: 10 Tips for Using Love to Make Your Life Happier and Easier

As we've observed, love is the highest-frequency energy in the Universe. It is the positive energy that drives and powers the Universe. When you raise your own personal frequency to match the Universe, you will be floating along in concert with the Universe instead of going against it. In other words, you have the opportunity to grab your board and go *Surfing the Love Vibration*.

So how does one grab the wave?

- Whenever you are confronted with an unpleasant situation or conflict, send love as your advance guard. Stop before you speak. Instead imagine sending out pink light from your heart or throwing a net of love over the participants.

- Before you enter a situation you think might be confrontational, shower yourself in pink light. Feel yourself being loved and embraced by the people you are soon to encounter.

- When you feel down, depressed, unworthy, unloved, or unattractive, give yourself a love bath! You are a fabulous human being, a part of the Universe's essence. Remember that you are loved and that you must love yourself. By doing so, you will attract more love.

- Love those who you often forget to love. People such as mailmen, auto mechanics, or store clerks who make your life easier and provide service to you.

- Forgive and love difficult relatives, ornery neighbors, demanding bosses, forgetful boyfriends, nagging wives, bad waiters, clueless salesclerks, crabby seniors, and anyone else that has been an annoyance in your life previously. Love them until they begin picking up your "vibe" and begin behaving differently!

- Choose love first when you must have a heart-to-heart talk with your loved ones—no matter what the topic. Start from that framework, not from anger, disappointment, or need. Don't accuse or demand. Seek compromise.

- Practice random acts of kindness. Whether it's for someone you know or someone you don't, such acts of grace are a powerful message of love in the Universe.

- When you feel fear, seek its opposite. Are you afraid of success or failure?

Practical Conscious Creation Tip No. 42

Becoming Aware of Love

As we go about our days, we often become insensitive to the power of love in our lives. With all of the other pressures that build up, we often take love for granted. We also sometimes lose sight of our ability to Consciously Create more love in our lives. I have begun doing an exercise that I want to share with you as it might help you attract more love in your life and remember to appreciate what you already do have. Each day, under the heading of "How I Have Given or Received Love Today," I record at least 10 ways that I have given or received love that day. It could be a friend who signs off a phone call saying "I love you and miss you," to hugging my neighbor's cat. It might be loving myself by putting an extra conditioner in my hair to make it extra soft. It could be listening intently to my brother talk about the important transitions in his life. Perhaps it's letting someone do something nice for me that I usually insist on doing myself. It might be comforting a friend or family member in pain. By consciously opening ourselves to give and receive love, we are telling the universe that we are ready, willing, and available for more—and it is amazing how many ways we discover we are already blessed by small acts of love that we take for granted!

Are you afraid of trying something new? Are you afraid to voice your feelings? Whatever you fear can be transformed with love. Give yourself love and permission. Trust the Universe to help you, once you've administered that love.

• When in doubt, spout love! Not sure what to do or how to handle something? Just send out waves of love. Direct them toward anyone who impacts you and your decision. Direct them toward the desired outcome. Direct them toward yourself. Direct them toward the Universe.

• Love the World! Love the earth and its inhabitants—all living things. Love the people who are courageous and conscious leaders. Love the people that put their lives on the line to protect us (police, firefighters, servicemen and women, search & rescue). Love the people who live a conscious life—and love those who don't so that they may become conscious and caring. Love the animals, sea creatures, and insects that share our earth. Love the food and water that sustains us. Love truth and integrity. Respect everyone, so that they may become the social engine that drives the world forward.

Love, Not Judge

For most of us, judging ourselves and others is an ingrained everyday habit that we may not even be aware that we do. It's just a way of life.

We gossip about other people. We assign value to individuals before we even speak to them, determining if they are worthy of our time. We make assumptions about people by virtue of their skin color or the work that they do. We complain about our co-workers, colleagues, relatives, lovers and, even friends! We are critical of the way people do things, what they think, how they talk, who they hang out with and what decisions they make in their lives.

We judge things that happen to us, from experiences we have to opportunities that come our way. Everything is either good or bad, and when we do judge it to be bad, our response is not one of acknowledgement and discernment, but rather worry, fret, fear, disappointment, or annoyance. In other words, we assign negative connotations and attach negative vibrations to things we cannot change—things that have already happened and are past.

It's not just other people that we behave in this way toward; when it comes to ourselves, we are almost inevitably overcritical and judgmental. How often have you thought of yourself as not good enough, not smart enough, not accomplished enough, not attractive enough, not appealing enough, not fit enough, not healthy enough, not outgoing or adventurous enough, not graceful or feminine enough, not masculine enough? Before long, you really believe those things about yourself. You create your reality.

Judgment is everywhere in our lives. Wouldn't it be easier if we just accepted everything! Imagine if we could embrace everyone and every experience with equanimity, and our experiences as simply the observation of an observer— "Oh isn't that interesting?"—instead of immediately sizing them up and being critical. We would then meet every new person and experience with a welcoming energy and intention. If an experience complicates our life, we would simply see it as a valuable "redirection"—the Universe showing us that it is time to find alternatives, or that we must try harder to find a new approach. No action is inherently good or bad—it just is!

After wrestling with many of these issues myself, I created a new mantra. This affirmation has helped me greatly and I want to pass it along to you. When I find myself judging someone, myself, or an experience, I simply repeat to myself the phrase, *"Love, Not Judge!"*

This is an ideal reminder that if I choose to vibrate love instead of judgment, it automatically opens me up to acceptance. By opening myself to acceptance, I stand to receive more love. It's a wonderfully perfect circle! And when I open myself up to acceptance, I become a powerful magnetic force for spiritual blessings and material benefits. When that happens, we're really humming along!

So I encourage you to try it on everything!

— That food you were served by your host was a bit too spicy? *Love, Not Judge!*

— The suit your favorite uncle is wearing at Christmas is pretty ratty? *Love, Not Judge!*

— Your boyfriend gave you a sweater you cannot see yourself wearing? *Love, Not Judge!*

— You note the love handles on your hips and wrinkles on your face? *Love, Not Judge!*

— Your boss is often demanding and unyielding? *Love, Not Judge!*

Practical Conscious Creation Tip No. 43

Help the People You Love Experience Their Dreams

I recently had an opportunity to see a troupe of Rat Pack Imitators. It brought back some important memories for me of the time that I took my mother to see Frank Sinatra and Sammy Davis Jr. in a live concert. My parents had been great fans of those wonderful entertainers nicknamed The Rat Pack, and had seen them multiple times in Las Vegas. But once my dad had passed on, I chose to do some special things just for my mom with the intention of helping her realize her dreams. One of those was to see Sinatra and Davis once again, and so we did. Another was to visit all of the places in the United Kingdom that she had read about in her favorite novels—so we went to London, Bath, Brighton, and Edinburgh. She wanted to fly first class once in her life, so I took her to New York and upgraded so we could sit in first class. We went to the Museum of Radio and TV to watch favorite family TV shows, long off the air. And there were many other special moments. My point is this: I helped my mom live her modest dreams and in the doing, allowed us to create great memories that will forever stay with me. When she passed on, I had absolutely no questions as to whether I had done enough, whether she knew I loved her, or whether I had given her the quality time she craved. So while your loved ones are still here, make sure that you help make their dreams come true and share those experiences with them. It will give you peace of mind.

— Your wife asked you to stop by the store on your way home—again? *Love, Not Judge!*

— You are stuck in traffic and running late for a meeting? *Love, Not Judge!*

— You didn't get that proposal of marriage you so desperately wanted? *Love, Not Judge!*

— You weren't invited to the cool kids' party? *Love, Not Judge!*

— Your crop of garden tomatoes just didn't make it this year? *Love, Not Judge!*

Let go of judgment and open yourself to accept using this magic little mantra. It is amazing the transformation that this phrase can create. Maybe not overnight, but it will unfold. When you get in the habit of spotting your negative critical judgments, and consciously eradicating them, you begin to raise your personal frequency. When you add the element of love and acceptance, then miracles happen!

So tuck this phrase in your pocket, hold it in your heart, stick it on your mirror and your computer, and write it on a piece of paper in your wallet. Do whatever you have to do to remind yourself that you have a choice of being a judge or being an accepting force for love!

The Compassion Quotient

Do you think of yourself as compassionate? How do you react when you see someone on the street begging for money or work? How do you respond when your aging parent complains about never seeing you? What happens in your mind when you view thousands displaced after earthquakes in Third World countries? What is your response when you observe a child crying?

Do you take a bare notice and rush on with your busy life, or perhaps think, "At least that's not me." Maybe you have a moment of reflection and a small feeling of care or concern—and then focus on something else.

As our lives become so complicated and the emotional demands on us so intense, what has been lost is compassion. Whether that takes the form of a kind word, a wish for better circumstances for the unfortunate, or an act undertaken to comfort or aid someone, we can each do more. Compassion, a vibrational form of love, is in short supply. We are quick to give money and slow to give of ourselves.

So what is your Compassion Quotient and how can you increase it? Keep in mind that the more you give, the more you will get when you need it.

- Are you oblivious to others' pain, loss, and longing?

- Are you only a little bit compassionate? You remember to call on someone's birthday but you have to be prompted to call your sick relative?

- Do you feel anguish when you see someone fall in the street and go over to help? Do you comfort someone in obvious emotional pain?

- Do you reach out to someone you know who is suffering in silence and take them to get help? Do you offer aid and a kind word to a homeless person? Do you comfort someone who has lost his or her home due to financial reversals?

- Do you volunteer to help strangers in need in your community? Are you unfailingly kind and willing to listen to the elderly, regardless of how cantankerous they can become?

- Are you always on call for family members in a crisis—but available even when it isn't a crisis?

- Do you get on an airplane and head across the country to help with a rescue mission? Do you take in an unwanted child to your home? Do you expend your own love, time, and money to help someone who is not related to you?

Upping your Compassion Quotient requires being in your heart, not in your head. Here are a few key steps:

- Stop and feel. Don't just let it pass through you. Feel for that person. Be empathetic.

- Consciously Create a reserve of love, warmth, and kindness within yourself and hold a vision for healing for the other person or people.

- Be compassionate to the person in need.

- Ask what you can do. Help without asking, if you know what needs to be done.

- Be available to those who are lonely, who are in need, or who are without resources. Sometimes a kind word is as valuable as a gold coin.

Practical Conscious Creation Tip No. 44

Attracting the Friends You Want

As you begin traveling a more conscious and high-fre-quency path, you may discover that many of your friends no longer seem right for your life—or they may not feel comfortable with the changes you are making. Negative people, in particular, can consistently pull you back into old habits and can just lower your mood or create irrita-tion. If you decide to spend less time with them, you may find a void in your life, which may in turn lead to a sense of loneliness. So here's an important idea. . . Consciously Create the kind of new friends that you *do* want: people who share your embodiment of love and joy. It's some-thing that I did. I asked the Universe to present me with new like-minded, high-frequency friends. And now my cup runneth over with amazing, loving, supportive, giv-ing, caring, grateful, and kind people who are all focused on making their immediate world and the world at large better for their presence. And it happened within just a couple of months from the point of my asking for it! I feel truly blessed that my request—my conscious intention—was made manifest in such an incredibly rich way. Do try it yourself!

- Commit to doing something weekly to help someone you don't know. Pay it forward.

- Volunteer when there is a crisis in your community. Reach out with your heart. *Be* compassion, don't just *do* compassionate acts. Show others how to be compassionate; some people just don't know how, and they learn by observation.

- Be compassionate toward yourself. It will make you more compassionate toward others.

- Forgive—a lot! Forgiveness is compassion for you and for the person you are forgiving.

- Be compassionate for the world and for both its sufferers and for those committing the acts that create suffering. Compassion—feeling love and respect for someone and expressing that love and respect—is the only true way to resolve the planet's problems.

May you grow to have a 100 percent Compassion Quotient!

Living in a Love-Centered Society

Have you ever wondered what life would be like if we lived in a Love-Centered Society? If Love were the most valuable commodity instead of money and possession?

This amazing Utopia would mean that we would exalt those who show the most compassion, humility, and selflessness—instead of celebrities and the wealthy. Instead of being competitive, we would actually strive to cooperate. Imagine that! Each of us would work for the good of the whole, so that abundance could increase for all of us. No more "me first!"

In a love-centered society, no one would be homeless and the aged would be cared for. Parents would rear their children with such care and thoughtful awareness that those children would not seek solace in drugs, alcohol, and sex. With such love between partners, family abuse would disappear.

In a love-centered society, we would strive to rehabilitate those who have broken the law. People of all different cultures would share the wealth of their individual cultures with the wider society. Society itself would be multicultural and multiracial,, because there would be no barriers to love.

In a love-centered society, we would recognize the humanity in everyone. We would realize that we are truly one great energy compartmentalized temporarily in individual human frames: By giving love to one, we are giving love to all.

In a love-centered society, we would extend that love to all the living beings on the planet and to the earth itself. We would treat them with kindness, compassion, common sense, and respect.

In a love-centered society, we would love ourselves so that we can fully love others, and we would teach love to all our offspring and everyone influenced by us. We would set an example of being a loving force in the world.

In a love-centered society, we would presume another's innocence, accept responsibility for our own actions, encounter others with trust in our hearts, work to alleviate dissension or dis-alignment with others, and engage in a relationship with love as the true outcome—and not ownership or control.

In a love-centered society, we would love our bodies and take care of them so that our health radiates. We address discord in ourselves and with others quickly so that emotional blocks evaporate and leave a loving and free flow of energy coursing through us.

In a love-centered society, each of us would adhere to our conscience, open ourselves to the wisdom and guidance of the Universe, and use love as the guiding principle for all decisions in our lives.

In a love-centered society, success would not be measured by how much money you have accrued; instead, it would be measured by whether you've lived a life of love, joy, and compassion, and how loved and uplifted others feel around you—how far your love light shines.

I don't know about you, but I'm working on my little part of the world right now, creating my little love-centered corner. I'm putting love first as my new life commitment. Care to join me? How about we then link up our love-centered neighborhoods and see what wonders can occur!

Practical Conscious Creation Tip No. 45

Don't Wait Till They Are Gone!

This week I had a note from a dear friend to say that she and her husband are retiring from their teaching jobs and moving from California to New Mexico. It was a shock! I had thought I had another year or two before they retired to visit them only an hour away. But economics being what they are, the high school district offered them a great buy-out a year early, and they took it. That made me realize how much time I *haven't* spent with them when I could have. . . and now they will be going away. There are two positive aspects in this. First, I do have a few months in which I can go visit before they leave. Second, I now have a place to visit in Las Cruces! But this experience reminded me that our time with the people that illuminate our spirit is often on our back burner. Make spending time with your dear friends a front-burner priority! It's a decision you'll always be happy you made.

Chapter 8

Romance and Relationships

Applying Conscious Creation techniques to romance and relationship is one of the most visible transformative paradigms. There are uncountable extraordinary stories about people who change themselves and suddenly their partners are willing, reinvigorated and collaborative. Applying your positive energy toward enhancing a relationship or attracting a new one can have happy, life-altering consequences.

How to Stay Positive With a Negative-Vibration Spouse or Partner

People who are making the change to a conscious and spiritually-driven life often discover that they are yoked to someone who is not prepared to come along on that journey. The partner is mired in his or her own negative thoughts and emotions, and meets any topic of spiritual enlightenment, positive vibration, and Conscious Creation with a wall of resistance.

Don't despair: lots of others have gone through this phase, too, and come out on the other side with a happier life. Let's look at what you can do in this situation:

- **Stay in your positive vibration state.** Don't allow your spouse or mate to pull you out of alignment with the Universe. When you feel yourself drawn into it, take a walk, go play with the kids, read a book, go have lunch with your best friend… and continue to think and feel positive about yourself, your life and the good qualities in your partner.

- **Create a sacred place in your home where you can go to meditate, clear your chakras, express gratitude, Consciously Create, connect with the Universe—activities that keep your frequency high.** Ask your partner to respect this private time, so that you can "recharge." This recharging should continue to buttress you against his or her negativity.

- **Demonstrate how your life has changed by just being happier, more up-beat, less stressed.** Soon your partner may want to know what it is that has changed you and how he/she can get some of it!

- **By changing how you respond to things, your spouse is bound to adjust.** If you are doing something different, that will change the dynamic between you and within the family. Your partner will have to adapt in some ways to meet or stay up with the new you.

- **Visualize a harmonious relationship.** See your relationship changing and your partner opening up to greater dialogue, a more open-minded attitude and a willingness to explore new avenues—new ways of thinking. Take your focus off of what is WRONG, and put it on what is right and what you desire.

- **Throw your "love net" around him or her.** I really believe this is an empowering tool to create waves of love that generate vibrational change. See yourself throwing the net of positive loving energy over your mate and yourself so that it will allow him/her to release the negativity in a net of safety and acceptance. This change raises the vibration between the two of you, flooding him or her with your loving, positive energy.

- **Each day of the week, spend five minutes telling your partner one or more of the things you love about him or her.** Your partner will be delighted to hear praise instead of complaints! It may well begin to shift his/her expectations, mood and outlook.

- **Focus on making the present moment the very best and most enjoyable you can, while creating your vision for the future.** Release the past. Don't reintroduce old patterns, hold him or her to past behavior by bringing up how it's been previously, and make sure that you don't fall back into old, negative, repetitive interactions yourself. Let go of the anticipation that your partner will respond in "the same old way." Leave the door open for change and possibility. Create a new pattern of interaction through your change of emotions, thoughts and energy habits.

- **Present your partner with positive alternatives.** When he or she focuses on the negative, gently demonstrate what alternative thought, emotion, or perception may further his or her desire. Be a teacher, but do it gently, don't force-feed these concepts.

- **Become a Master Manifestor.** As you raise your frequency, good things will increasingly come to you at your beckoning. If your spouse or partner gets jealous, point out that he/she can do this too if he/she follows your path. Then hand your partner a copy of *The Art of Conscious Creation,* or this book, or some other book on conscious manifesting! Accept that the Universe is creating an opportunity to test how effectively you can maintain your own positive energy in the face of a challenge!

- **Lastly—and this is the most extreme outcome—if you have tried all of these over time and you find yourself in a situation that is not emotionally healthy for you, you may have to leave the relationship.** It is when the negatives outweigh the positives, with little prospect for change, that you have a responsibility to your ebullient and joyful soul to find an alternative lifestyle either alone or with a more positively disposed and spiritually aware partner. Remember, even when there are children involved, they fare better with at least one happy parent, rather than two miserable ones. For most relationships, however, the awakening of one partner is often the key to evolution and positive growth for both. May yours be one of those!

Practical Conscious Creation Tip No. 46

Supportive Listening

Don't you just want to jump in and fix someone's life when you see them doing things you don't agree with? It's so easy just to tell them what they should do. Especially children, spouses, and people you are close to. When you live in close proximity to someone, you feel as if they are almost an extension of you, and you are more likely to be critical—because by fixing them, you fix part of your life. But the problem is: You CAN'T fix their life. And if you push your ideas on them, you will only find resistance and pushback. Try listening and encouraging instead. Ask questions. Let that person talk. Show you support him or her regardless of whether you agree with the path that person is taking. Show confidence that he or she will ultimately make decisions that will lead to growth and success. And in your mind, Consciously Create a happy and fulfilled person, giving that individual the space to grow and thrive, whatever path she or he follows. You'll be surprised at how this will change the relationship for the better and erase the tension and strain for both of you.

Ten Steps for Attracting Love

The image is culturally iconic: the cherubic Cupid pointing his bow and arrows at his soon-to-be victims, smiting them with love. But as much as this sweet image has been part of our cultural legacy, it needs an update! Cupid needs to add particle and wave physics to his arsenal! The little guy needs to attract instead of attack!

All that said, you're probably not waiting around for Cupid to do you any favors. If you are a single person today, you are more likely to be searching for love at an online dating service (Match.com, EHarmony.com, and so on), through social networking (Facebook, My Space, and the like), at work (where statistics show a high percentage of relationships begin), in school, at your gym/yoga studio, or within your special interest group (church/spiritual center, pet rescue, cycling club, cause-related organization, and so on). Or maybe you've just given up looking, but not given up hope.

Love is possible for any and all of us. However, we need to begin to view the search for love in terms of Conscious Creation and energy—a far more effective and compelling way now that we understand more about the Law of Attraction and energy management.

So, how would you go about attracting a soulmate, a true love? Let's look at ways to apply your skills at Conscious Creation. Here are 10 steps.

1. **Raise your personal frequency.** In order to be attractive to a prospective partner you must be vibrating positive, compassionate, appreciative, loving frequencies. If you are vibrating negative waves of energy (desperation, resentment at past lovers, judgment, criticism, self-centeredness, low self-esteem, and so on), you will drive people away even if your words are sweet. People will sense what lies beneath because your body will be radiating that energy. Furthermore, if you raise your frequency, you will become a faster and more effective manifestor, attracting your partner more quickly.

2. **Become love to attract love.** Like attracts Like. If you want to attract love, you must vibrate love—unconditional love. You must be loving in intent, in your heart, in deed, in action, in appearance. Loving energy should permeate your entire being. Get quiet and allow love to become your default energy.

3. **Love yourself.** If you are constantly self-critical (I'm not thin enough, I'm too bald, I wish I was smarter or more glib with the opposite sex, and so on), you are vibrating energies that will repel your prospective lover. It follows: if you are critical of yourself, you will be critical of him/her. If you accept and love yourself, you have begun the process of accepting your partner for who he or she is. Furthermore, if you dislike yourself or find fault, you are not operating in a state of unconditional love. It is thus highly likely that you could attract someone who is equally insecure or whose love is just as conditional. Love yourself unconditionally and you generate the frequency to attract unconditional love.

4. **Start Consciously Creating love.** Create a vision of the person you want to bring into your life. Not just what he or she might look like, but what qualities that person has, what interests might you share, what values, and how the relationship will *feel* to you. When you start Consciously Creating, remember that the emotional component is most critical for this is the "express mail to the cosmic post office." You must feel the emotions of living this beautiful relationship.

5. **Be specific.** It is essential that you be specific in your Conscious Creation about what you desire in your soulmate. My friend Lee is a very handsome, charming, intelligent, and successful entertainment entrepreneur, but he had difficulty finding the right woman. So he sat down and started writing, getting very specific about what he wanted in a wife. Very soon after that she walked into his life, and they have now been blissfully married more than a dozen years. The Universe can't bring it forth if you are unspecific or conflicted. It has to have clarity to match the vibrational request.

6. **Make space in your life for your lover.** Is there room in your life for this lover? Is there enough time in your life? Is there enough "attention bandwidth" to make someone feel valued? Is there space in your closets? Create spiritual and energetic space so that the Universe can fill the vacuum with the partner you are seeking. This also applies to releasing old energies relating to past partners. If you hold onto bad memories, anger, resentment, and other negative emotions, this energy will not allow positive, new loving energy to come forth. Dump the garbage and let the Universe fill up your psychic space with the vibrant, loving energy inspired by your relationship with a wonderful new partner.

7. **Trust the Universe.** Have faith that once you start this process, and you have done all the aforementioned steps, that the Universe is at work cre-

Practical Conscious Creation Tip No. 47

It's So Touching. . .

Touching is a spiritual experience. Oftentimes people are too self-conscious to touch others or let them touch you. Thus, hugging is an occasional occurrence. But touching is a powerful exercise in Conscious Creation. It allows you to pass your love, affection, admiration, gratitude, and appreciation in a visceral way. The more you touch, the more you send waves of your positive frequency out into the world. . . and the more will boomerang back to you. So hug your neighbor. Caress the shoulder of that elderly person in your life. Kiss the children you encounter. Hold hands with your best friend. And make love by touching the face of your lover. Touch is your energy's forward guard.

ating a new reality for you, presenting you with opportunities to connect with possible partners, maneuvering you into situations where the right person may present him or herself. Believe that you will meet your partner and you will. . . but note that this will be in divine timing. It may not be on your timetable. So be patient.

8. **Use affirmations.** Create and restate affirmations that reinforce your belief and readiness for this person's arrival. Statements like: "I willingly embrace the loving partner who is coming into my life and am creating a safe haven in my life for him/her," or "I am filling myself with abundant and unconditional love so that I may share it with my lover who is now in my life." It is especially effective to act as if that person has already arrived on your doorstep when creating affirmations.

9. **Prepare for love.** Take the steps to prepare yourself for love. Be groomed beautifully, even when running errands. Take pride in your appearance. Pamper your body. Work on your fitness. Make your home welcoming. Take classes to enhance your knowledge and wisdom. Practice your charm, kindness, and focused attention on others so that you will be accustomed to doing so when your partner arrives.

10. **Raise your antenna for love.** Be out in the world. Don't isolate yourself. Raise your antenna and use your wavelengths of energy to start connecting with people. Put yourself in places where you might meet someone—or someone who can introduce you to someone else. Let your waves go out and bring back your new love—just like a modern wave-wielding Cupid.

Travels With Your Beloved

It's summer vacation time—a time when many couples go away to enjoy romantic sunsets, make memories, and explore new adventures. Which leaves many of us single people feeling pretty left out. But if we dwell on that feeling, than we just attract more loneliness—or "stay-at-home aloneness."

But what if I told you that I have a wonderful way for you to manifest both your wonderful new beloved and your romantic getaway at the same time?

It's a practice I've begun this year to open my mind, my heart, and my energy to the vibration that would create a future filled with fantastic world travels with the man who is to be my loving companion.

It's called "Traveling with Your Beloved." Download a simple online calendar template where you can write a few words in each square. Then go buy or dig out a bunch of travel magazines, the travel sections of your daily paper, or go hunting on travel websites.

Each day you create a fabulous vacation in your mind with your ideal lover—some place you've never been, but have read about in your research. I keep a file of great places I want to go, and so this process fits in perfectly.

Now, you want to create this vision with all the reality you can muster. See it. See the beauty, the colors, the quaint buildings, the colorful local people, the romantic vistas, the pretty outdoor cafes, and so on. Smell its smells—the ocean, foods cooking, the perfume of the flowers. Hear the sounds—waves lapping, swooshing skis, birds chirping, lions roaring. Touch what there is to touch—the soft back of a manta ray, the textiles, the roses, the wood carvings.

You will then begin to experience all this alongside of your sweet love. Experience the things you want to do together—sightseeing, sailing, cycling, dining, dancing, touching, laughing, reading, or making love.

So pick a place. Then start to fill in the picture from the moment you arrive. Where are you staying? What's the view from the window? How does he or she nuzzle your ear while you look out the window together? What does the room look like? Is there a breeze wafting in from the windows? What do you two first want to do or see?

Head out the door and begin your adventure—museums; photography; walking around and exploring; hiking, cycling, snorkeling, diving, horseback riding, rafting, or skiing; going to traditional ethnic restaurants, local drinking establishments, or cafes; listening to music; following in the footsteps of history; lying on a beach; experiencing nature; watching beautiful sunsets; meditating together; and so on. Remember to picture the interaction between you—hand holding, kissing, snuggling, hugging, eyes locking, laughter, feeding each other sweets. . .

Now imagine coming back to the room at the end of the day. What happens between you? Go ahead. It's your dream. You can do anything you want!

Be imaginative from beginning to end. It can be as exotic or as mundane as you want. Do you want to go to Antarctica and live below ground in winter for a week? Or take a weekend away at Big Sur in California, sail the

Practical Conscious Creation Tip No. 48

Mirror Reading

When I engage in dialogue with people who become angry, short, and irritated, I look to see if I had any hand in their response or reaction. Certainly their type of emotional response stems from their own issues; it is not my responsibility to resolve their personal relationship with themselves or their past. However, people can be an excellent mirror for determining whether we are projecting our negative energy outward—energy that may indeed trigger an exaggerated or unnecessary response. Were my own unconscious words and energy attracting a negative response from the person? If I had chosen different words, a different tone of voice, or a different energy to enter the encounter, would I have gotten a different result? If I hadn't felt tired and frustrated, had smiled instead of looking impatient to get out of there, if I had asked instead of barked my request to the clerk, would he have snapped back or carelessly torn the shopping bag with my merchandise spilling all over? Use others as a mirror to remind yourself to mind your own personal frequency! This is especially true in relationships.

Caribbean, or float the Amazon? Then of course, there's the French Riviera or an African Safari. Your imagination is the only limit.

Here are a few places I've already been with my love (in my mind, of course). . . Singapore; a Greek Island; Vermont in the autumn; Provence, France; Angkor Wat, Cambodia; Rio de Janeiro, Brazil; Sophia, Bulgaria; Canary Islands; Tierra del Fuego, Argentina; Catalina Island, California; the Galapagos Islands; and Washington DC.

Do this every day for a year and record on your calendar where you have been. By doing this, you have created the emotion of love each day in your heart, and set the energy in motion to attract prospective partners to you who share your love of travel and the world. And just maybe, next summer, you'll be among those traveling with your beloved for real!

Conscious Communication

Relationships grow or fade based on how effective the communication is between parties. If individuals are adamant about their point of view, it is unlikely that disputes can be resolved without a painful verbal battle and hard feelings. Needing to be right is one of the most destructive forces in any communication. Seldom are anybody's needs met when people cannot reduce the level of rhetoric to a point where they can truly listen to the other party or put themselves in the other person's shoes.

"Conscious Communication" is a means of helping people deal with conflict and differing needs in a spiritual and loving manner. While it can be used with any two people, it is particularly effective with people in highly emotionally-charged personal relationships. If put into practice on a regular basis, it prevents discussions from escalating into pitched battles and allows for solutions to evolve. Most importantly, it enables trust to return to a relationship—trust that each person will honor the sacredness of the other individual's dignity.

• First, set an intention for you to be the means of introducing your partner to this new form of loving communication and that your partner responds willingly. Use your powers of Conscious Creation to see the two of you using this form to develop a foundation of loving communication for the duration of your relationship.

- Stay conscious of sensitive topics and patterns of dialogue that have led to arguments in the past. Before they move into stage two, propose to your partner that you switch over to your Conscious Communication technique.

- If things heat up before you've had a chance to implement your Conscious Communication technique, don't react in anger, even if you are angry. Say to your partner, "Since our relationship is so important to me, and I love you so deeply, I don't want to react in anger. Let's set an appointment now—for a time later today—which will allow us to calm down, and we can explore what we are feeling in our Conscious Communication process." Then set up the appointment.

- Don't spend the rest of the time stewing. Instead explore in your mind the issues that are so meaningful to you and that underlie your anger. Ask for guidance if you need it.

- Begin your Conscious Communication process by getting deeply into your heart and opening your soul. Be calm and open to Source speaking through you. Ask your partner if he/she is willing to do the same.

- Then say to your partner, "I love you so much and want to honor both of us in this process. We are opening a safe dialogue where we can be honest with each other. In this Conscious Communication, I want to tell you how I feel about this issue, how I perceive this from my point of view, and then I want to hear your viewpoint and how that makes you feel. Please listen first and hear me out and then I will do the same for you."

- As you then explain your point of view, begin first with statements about how you are feeling, such as: "This is how this experience/issue makes me feel. . . , " "I am sad because. . . ," "I am hurt because. . . , " "I am feeling unappreciated because. . . ," "I am feeling unloved because. . . , " Never accuse the other party or say, "You did or didn't do such and so " Make your expression specifically about the impact it is having on *you*. Your emotions are not up for debate. It's your personal experience, so it should not be threatening to your partner. It forces him/her to feel what you are feeling.

- Then state what your perception is or was. "Here is how I perceived what occurred." Remember his/her perception may be very different from yours.

- Then, encourage your partner to respond next. You may be very surprised to learn that what you thought was happening with him/her was not what he or she was truly experiencing.

Practical Conscious Creation Tip No. 49

The Blame Game

If you find yourself blaming someone else for anything, stop immediately! Remember that you are responsible for what happens in your life, whether you are aware of it or not. Look first at what you might have done to create the situation or failed to do and allowed the situation to develop. Consider what you might change or release yourself, and watch what happens in the dynamics of the relationship once you make the transformation. Don't be surprised to see the other person change as well, as a result of you altering your resonance. You can also use this as a teaching opportunity with the other person or people, rather than assigning blame. Lastly, if the other party regularly fails to live up to his or her responsibilities after having been presented with an opportunity to transform, look at ways to release this person, rather than blaming him or her. It's within your hands to adjust, change, or release.

- Listen with your heart, not your head. Be compassionate, be understanding, be willing and open. Put yourself in his/her shoes. Try to see it from your partner's perspective.

- Acknowledge your appreciation for his/her willingness to reveal feelings and be honest. If that which was expressed is a surprise, be forthcoming and say, "I never knew you felt that way. Thank you for allowing me to understand what's going on in your head and your heart."

- Now offer, "So let's see if we can find a middle ground. Here is a change I think I can make. Will that work for you? And what change do you think you can make so that we can find a workable solution that can at least partly meet both of our needs."

- By making the first offer, you have shown good faith that this is indeed a dialogue designed to solve the problem *and not place blame*. You've proven it is a safe place for your partner to let his or her guard down and express feelings. Remember when someone expresses feelings, it makes that person even more vulnerable for greater hurt. But if you can create this ongoing sacred space for dialogue, trust will grow, along with harmony.

- As you conclude, reiterate your love for the other party and your intention to work to keep the balance. Remind him or her that if further negotiation is needed, it can again be refined using this same Conscious Communication technique. And follow through with that intention if things break down, instead of complaining, nagging, belittling, or raising your voice.

If both parties truly want the relationship to work and they are willing to take responsibility for their own emotions and perspective—and to listen to the other person's side of things—this Conscious Communication technique will be a vital gift to the partnership.

Chapter 9

Wealth and Prosperity

One of the most tangible signs that you are becoming an effective Conscious Creator is when you see a change in your bank account or your flow of income. Money is not and should not be the sole measurement of your success, but it certainly demonstrates that you are headed in the right direction. When money arrives easily and effortlessly, without the struggle that is often associated with revenue generation, then you are benefiting from the practices you have absorbed from these pages. May you prosper in all ways that enrich your life!

A Dialogue Between You and Your Money

I know this sounds strange, but it's time you started talking to your money. If you are feeling strapped, then you need to develop an up-close-and-personal relationship with your money. And when I say "your money," it may be money already in your bank or dollars that are on the way and you have yet to deposit in your account.

So let's start a dialogue between you and your money. What would you like to say to it? How do you want to make it feel? Do you appreciate it? Do you enjoy it? Do you love it? Are you grateful for the things it's helping you do— pay your bills, get a manicure, give gifts to your children, pay for the car repair, buy dinner for your best friend? It's fantastic, isn't it? It's just a tangible method to track the exchange of services and energy between people, but it's just so green! Green represents abundance, harmony, rebirth, and growth! Money lets you celebrate the success of your work life. It enables lots of forms of joyful entertainment. It provides enriching food.

So talk to your money. Romance it. Love it. Just like you would a puppy or a kitten.

What do you imagine it would like to say to you?

I love being able to service you.

I love being YOUR money and letting you pass me along to someone else to help make their life better.

I love making you feel good when you see lots of dollars fill up your bank account. Please spend me smartly and save me for a rainy day.

It's just so fun to bring joy, happiness, and prosperity to you!

Now what would you say to the money that has yet to arrive?

I'm so looking forward to your arrival.

Thank you for helping me to grow and prosper.

I promise to use you for my personal growth, for making wise choices and for helping others.

You're a blessing on the way, since I know that you'll help me pay down my mortgage quicker and will get me into a great place financially.

It will be so fun to have you by my side when I go to buy my new car, and get the wood and tools to build my son's treehouse.

Now I can take care of that treatment I need to get into peak health!

Oh and wonder of wonders, I can take that trip to Europe regardless of how the dollar is faring against the euro!

I am so thankful for your arrival!

Fun, isn't it? It's a unique way to Consciously Create your future wealth, employing joy, fun, and imagination, instead of intense focus on changing the future. This is a light-filled, joyous celebration of your wealth today—and a celebration of wealth to come.

So what other imagination tools can you devise to attract money and keep it coming?

Try these:

- **Grow a money tree.** Imagine you have a money tree in your tummy. (I actually posted a picture of a money tree on the wall in front of my desk as a reminder. (If you would also like one, please visit *www.practicalconsciouscreation.com/moneytree* for your very own money tree image!) Now envision it growing inside of you and each time you need some money, you clip some of its $$$ leaves. And watch, they grow back! There's an unlimited supply!

- **Magnetize your aura.** Imagine your aura in brilliant colors all around you. Set the intention to magnetize it. Zap! Now you are a money magnet, and money is coming from all over to stick to you! Pluck one from your crown chakra. Oh there's another one I can grab right off my ankle. Those dollars are just arriving from all over the Universe!

- **Feed your genie in a bottle.** Go find a funky old lantern or bottle, something antiquey and fun. Imagine this is the bottle in which your genie lives and he (or she!) is there to grant your money wishes. See your genie bringing you that money whenever you want or need it. But make sure to feed your genie lots of love and gratitude to keep him or her feeling special about your relationship. He or she will keep trying to please you as long as he or she feels appreciated.

- **Fill your magic box.** Find a beautiful box that evokes lovely thoughts whenever you open it. Each night go over, open it up and put in your imaginary savings. Keep piling in dollars—and oh yes, now and then put in the real thing! (Now that's an idea!)

Practical Conscious Creation Tip No. 50

Is Your Stock Going Up or Down?

Is your stock going up or down? As the market dips and jobs disappear, are you focused on the stock market or on your own personal stock? What do you have that will buoy you in this environment? Optimism, gratitude, love, talent, intelligence, determination, vision, a willingness to collaborate, inner strength, integrity, creativity, intuition, and other gifts and positive values? If you focus on bringing these to the table, it doesn't matter what happens in the stock market. You will survive and thrive, and so will those whom you influence! Focus on your gifts. These are the true gold in your life.

- **Bathe in the light of your emerald gem.** This one has always been powerful for me: When my business was in trouble many years ago, this imagery helped turn my life around. Go outside in the sunshine. Imagine a stunning, deep, rich-green emerald in the sky above you. See beams of emerald green light shining down on you, knowing that this light represents abundance, prosperity, and safety. Let it warm your shoulders and caress your body. Feel financially secured and blessed by the rich green universal gemstone.

So the minute you start feeling poor, turn your mind to one of these lovely fantasies or talk to your money. I have no doubt you'll start to see a change in your fortunes.

Twenty Ways to Trigger Abundance

You're seeing your savings dwindling, and you're getting deeper in debt. Fear is dominating your days and depression your nights. Willingly or unwillingly, you're feeding that monster called "Lack." So let's call an audible, as they say in football, and switch plays right now. Let's start focusing on the end zone and the touchdown you are going to score by looking ahead, not behind.

Stick to your own game plan. Don't listen to the news and other negative reinforcement. Your game plan is your own and will put you in the plus column if you just keep heading down field. Focus on these 20 game-winning strategies to trigger prosperity and abundance in your life.

1. **Make a choice to be abundant.** Let go of all other limiting beliefs. Set your intention.

2. **Live the concept of unlimited abundance in your personal and professional life.** Abundance for all drives the worldwide economic engine. You can operate a business responsibly on a budget and at the same time leave the door open for expansion. Operate from prudence, not scarcity. Set an intention for growth at the same time that you build your budget. Create goals that have room for increased revenue. Take actions that show your confidence in the fact that unlimited abundance is headed your way, and is earmarked for your future and the future of the world. There are unlimited opportunities for you out there. You just have to allow yourself to be guided to them.

3. **Define prosperity for yourself.** More time? More freedom? Less stress? More money to spend on what? More ways to share your wealth?

4. **See the world as an opportunity, not a hostile environment.** Always view a challenge as a chance to create anew!

5. **Each day put the Law of Attraction to work on your behalf.** Make sure that you are operating on a high frequency with positive focus, acts and values—and make correction where it is not. If you are operating on a high frequency, you are resonating with the Universe's vibration and you should attract money, resources, and business that are in alignment with you and your highest good.

6. **Be open to change.** The Universe puts things in your path for a reason. Resistance chokes off the flow.

7. **Everything happens for a reason.** There are no accidents. No doubt you've heard this before. If you stay open to this guidance, you will engage greater prosperity and opportunity. For example, let go of continually challenging clients or projects because the Universe is trying to give you a message. There is something better that awaits. Make energetic room for it.

8. **Is your work right for you, or do you need to make a change?** If you hate your job, your energy is destroying its ability to produce revenue. Does your work match your passion? Do you like your clients? What can you do both energetically and action-wise to change this—change your attitude, try a more positive approach with others, be more grateful, ask to shift roles in the company, take on more or less responsibility, delegate further, ask to be treated differently, start looking for a new job, put in your resignation, start your own business? Don't hold onto a job because it's paying the bills. And if you get "downsized," count your blessings. Have faith there is a better opportunity if you open the door for it.

9. **Give great value.** You serve yourself when you serve others, both in business and personally. Let others spread the word about you, your commitment, and your generosity!

10. **Listen to your intuition.** The Universe is speaking through your spirit. If you ignore it, you'll miss opportunities, make the wrong decisions about utilizing money, or worse—find yourself in unpleasant circumstances.

11. **Don't ignore things!** Step up and take responsibility. If the bills are piling up, don't shove them in the drawer. Offer payment plans, talk to your

bank/creditors, and so on. Create an exit strategy to your "short term shortage." Unclog the energy by giving it a place to flow.

12. **Be open to where your abundance will come from.** It's not always just from your paycheck. Review positive opportunities for wealth that could be yours—even if they seem a bit far-fetched. Dreaming is more than dreaming, it begins the process of creation. Let go of preconceived notions about where your money is coming from. Think about money in new terms—trade out, barter, additional staff or support so you can do more and bring in more income.

13. **Be clear about what you want!** The Universe can't present it if you are confused, unsure, and unspecific. Focus on what you *do* want. Not the problems or the images of pending disaster you've built up in your mind—unless you want to attract that. Create your personal and professional goals with a strong vision of success. Put them in writing.

14. **When faced with a decision, do what feels good to you.** Your body will tell you if this is the right or wrong decision. Or whether you are operating out of fear instead of optimism, enthusiasm, and excitement. If you make a decision from fear, it will surely cause the results to be unsatisfying. You'll feel it clearly through butterflies or tightness in your abdomen, headaches, stiffness in your neck. Look for the signs. If it "feels" good, you are on the right path.

15. **Act with vigor and vision.** Take steps that demonstrate to the Universe that you are deserving of abundance and worthy of the world's largess. Through your actions, show your co-workers, friends, and family that you believe in the bounty that this world affords, and that you have faith in the Universe and in the future to create the opportunities for a better life, a better nation and a better world. Embrace that robust future by taking the first steps.

16. **Pay it forward.** Do good deeds and make generous overtures to others, simply asking the recipients to pay it forward. Create the energy that will heal and repair, and plant positive healthy seeds that will allow abundance to grow.

17. **Allow things to happen—surrender.** Follow the guidance; the signs will be there. The doors will open. You don't need to push. . . Let the Universe move the pieces on the chess board, with you as the King.

Practical Conscious Creation Tip No. 51

Bless Your Money!

The next time you wince when you pay a bill, or dread paying for something, note this feeling. It is one of the factors that contributes to your financial strain. Our conscious and unconscious dreads, fears, and anxieties about money constrict our flow of Conscious Creation. However, there is a simple, easy-to-remember way to open up that channel of abundance. Bless your money! Bless it when it comes in. Bless it when you pay a bill, knowing that you are contributing to economic liquidity. Bless it when you deliver it to the cashier, because you are helping to keep that business healthy so it can be there for your convenience. Bless it when you give it to anyone or provide it for any purpose because somewhere in the chain you are helping someone else in need earn food and shelter. Bless it because it's a joyful form of energy! (Money = a fair exchange of energy for a service or product.) Bless it when you give it away to help someone else. Bless it because it helps create your abundance. Just take out a dollar bill right now and kiss it! And say thanks for the grace it affords you.

Now just remember this whenever you have that sense of money pressure or lack! Instantly start blessing your money, and very possibly you will soon begin to see those dollars multiply! I see my bills in a whole different light since I began doing this! And I actually feel good about paying them!

18. **Remember how powerful you are!** You have the ability to create whatever you can conceive!

19. **Don't work all the time, and don't think about work all the time.** Enjoy the other parts of your life that bring you joy. It is your state of joy and fun that will allow your frequency to call forth the abundance that creates more joy.

20. **Create something new that excites you!** Find one thing that you love and can at least generate a little money right away. Your passion and enthusiasm will kickstart your positive energy and focus your attention on opportunity and forward motion. This will create momentum that will lead to greater success and prosperity. A little excitement goes a long way toward priming the pump!

The Source of Your Prosperity

I'll bet you think that your money comes from the company that pays you a salary or the clients that pay your consulting fees?

But you would be wrong about that. Your money and abundance of all kinds comes from The Universe—the unlimited Source of all things. This is a very important fact to remember. Because just as assuredly as The Source can create what you now have, it can create more!

It can also create less if you are greedy, sloppy with your money, unhappy about your life in general, mistrustful of the Universe, ungrateful, or filled with fear.

So let's look at this unlimited source of income. How does it create prosperity? It transforms positive intentional energy into the form of currency that we use as exchange in our world today—money! Energy is limitless, so the prospect of more wealth is limitless.

Even if you are living on a fixed income today, this doesn't mean that is all there is. Using your inspiration and your creativity, you can find other ways to bring in more, stretch what you have, change what you are currently doing, and open the door for something else.

And then there is the occasional surprise! An unexpected tax return or gift from a friend. A mistake in your favor by the bank. A medical reimbursement check. A leap in your mutual funds. An investment that's matured. A back child support payment. Someone wants to buy something you created and just hung on your wall. A girlfriend buys you a plane ticket to visit her in another city. Someone hands you a coupon in the store that they cannot use.

So if you would like to optimize your possibilities of attracting more abundance, here are certain keys to keeping the wellspring flowing:

1. **Radiate love and gratitude.** First and foremost be in a state of love and gratitude. When you are emitting these vibrations it creates a positive "receptor" for wealth and abundance. Most of all, be grateful for the money you have and any new money that comes to you. However, the more grateful you are for everything in your life, the more abundance you experience.

2. **Be in the flow.** Money is like water; it is always flowing. You just need to be in the right place and mindset to receive it. So spend every day creating the perfect garden to be watered by this flow. Be at peace. Start your day with a ritual that consciously puts you in the Universe's flow of positive energy—a beam or cone of golden light shining down upon you and surrounding you. Daily ask for this flow of light and love to shower you with grace. Do actions during the day that honor this flow. Maintain integrity and speak with your heart open with compassion spilling forth.

3. **Stay open.** Be open to being directed to new and other sources of income. Don't turn something down because it's different from what you now know comfortably, or it requires time and effort. The Universe may be presenting you with an opportunity. This is not to say you *must* do everything put in front of you, but at least give it careful consideration. New ideas and new opportunities can lead to new wealth.

4. **Remember that financial limitation is a temporary condition.** If you are moping about, feeling the economic crunch is a downward spiral that will create long-term deprivation in your life, cut it out *now*! Because if you feel that way, that's what you'll get. If on the other hand you consistently remember that financial limitation is a temporary condition, and that it can be reversed at any time, you're already on your road to recovery.

5. **Be confident in your ability to manifest.** The more confident you are that you are a fast and rapid manifestor, the more you will likely manifest money quickly and easily. Know that you have this ability and this power, and that wealth is headed your way! That confidence and wisdom primes the pump.

6. **Ask for guidance; seek inspiration.** If you don't have any good ideas about increasing your abundance, then ask for guidance and inspiration. You'll be surprised at what ideas might come to your mind or opportunities placed in your path. Take inventory of your skills, passions, and unique talents to see how you might make additional money in fun ways that satisfy your heart and soul.

7. **Create visualizations.** I always think of myself standing under a waterfall with the Universe pouring down abundance on my head. Money is just flowing everywhere. What visions can you create that place you in a situation to be saturated, blessed or in receipt of money?

8. **Install a Fountain in Your Home.** In the Chinese feng shui tradition, flowing water in or around the home is a means to increase the energy (chi) that attracts wealth. Find and buy an inexpensive floor or table-top fountain that keeps money flowing to you. (And make sure to close all the toilet seats in your house regularly since money will flow down the drain and out of your home if you don't!)

9. **Trust the Universe.** Once you express your desire for increased money and start taking action, have faith that the Universe is working on it, too. (But first, just undertake your own housekeeping to make sure you are not doing anything else that can keep that wealth at bay—including being in a state of fear or emitting other negative vibrations.) Go about your business and remember to trust.

10. **Remember and revere the true source of your wealth.** When you are pitching an account, or having a conflict with the executives in your company, remember that it is not they who are the source of your income. Always remember and revere the true source of your money, and this will serve you well. It releases your beholden-ness to anyone but the Universe. This allows you to make wise decisions and not decisions based on fear. And it keeps you in a proper state of gratitude and awe at the amazing Source that grants you the means to enjoy your life more fully!

Practical Conscious Creation Tip No. 52

In God We Trust

The words *In God We Trust* are printed on American banknotes. Every time you take a banknote from your wallet, invest great trust and love in your knowledge and awareness that money flows to you from the Source so that you can sprinkle it around the world for your abundance and the abundance of others. Feel enriched by being the conduit. It's not yours to keep. It's yours to spend!

Chapter 10

Business Life

Practicing Conscious Creation in the office can yield exponential results. Whether you are the boss, one of the management team or among the many employees who are crucial to a company's success, the application of your positive vibrational energy can impact the quality of the experience for yourself and your co-workers, company moral, customer or client satisfaction, your paycheck and the company bottom line. By applying your Conscious Creation skills at the workplace, you are sure to be happier, more creative and more satisfied at work—or you will make the right judgment to formulate or find a place where your gifts are appreciated.

The Conscious Creation Equation for Manifesting Success

Someone recently asked me why I know that I will be successful when I undertake something, and the answer popped into my head so clearly that it astonished me. My response to him was, "Because of four key factors. . . "

- I can envision the project in advance and see how I want it to unfold. I see it succeeding as I perceive it;

- I am willing to put in the effort that is required to bring it to fruition;

- I have faith in my intelligence, my intention to do something of value, my commitment to achieve it, and my good judgment that this fills a need;

- I have faith in the Universe and its willingness to respond to my desires and bring me what is in my highest good.

Or simply put:

Vision + Initiative + Faith in Self + Faith in Universe = Your Desired Outcome

I call this the Conscious Creation Equation for Manifesting Success. If you are practicing each of these concepts when you embark on a new endeavor, you will succeed. I have spent my life creating successful businesses, forming alliances, doing nonprofit work, and so on, by operating with these four elements as part of my day-to-day mindset. Let's look at each of them a bit closer.

Vision

If you conceive a vision of something you want to start, you must have a passion for it—or else why do it? So you already begin with the high vibration energies of "birth" and "passion." This gives any idea or project a great jump-start. But as you visualize it, you also place your focus on it. And as we know about the Universal Laws, what you focus upon is what you will manifest. By creating the high-frequency image in your mind and investing it with your emotion you are generating that "express mail package to the cosmic post office."

Initiative

When I first mentioned this equation to my friend, I used the term "hard work." But then, I took that back and rephrased it. Why work hard? That's absolutely not a necessity in the Universe that I am experiencing today. I can work smart. I can work with commitment. I can work with enthusiasm and passion. What I was trying to say was that I was willing to put in the initiative and the effort to make the project successful. But I can do that without "working hard!" There is no reason to make anything "hard," when we can work effectively and still work easily.

Faith in Self

This is a big one! People who believe in themselves tend to be very successful in all their endeavors. Each of us has great gifts, but to allow them to flower fully, you must appreciate and honor them with your belief. This is where you must actually take for granted how talented and smart you are—because the minute you start doubting, that's when you allow failure to creep in. Now we are each evolving spiritually at different rates, so you may feel confident professionally but have lower self-esteem in your personal self-view. Where you feel confident is where you will likely see your success. So start taking stock of your assets and being grateful for them. These are the beacons that shine on the path to your success.

Count up your past great achievements—don't overlook them. Build faith in yourself so you can use this as a springboard to future successes. Where are your skills—in your intellect, your creativity, your problem solving ability, your facility with people, your skill with numbers, your diplomacy, or perhaps your persistence? Keep your faith in yourself and you will be well rewarded.

Faith in the Universe

If you start from a premise that you are supported and that the Universe is just waiting to assist you in your success, you cannot fail. By demonstrating your faith, you are enabling the Universe to line up all the elements in your favor, unblocked by your own doubt, fear, or feeling of separation from the Source. What this also does is tell the Universe that you are open to guidance. If there is a flaw in your plan, the Universe will let you know; it will either tweak it on its own or steer you in a different direction. This high-frequency energy is a powerful ally that streamlines the path to success.

So this Conscious Creation Equation for Manifesting Success is very simple and unencumbered. You don't need to make it any more complicated than this if you want to ensure the success of your endeavors. Do the math—then toast your achievement!

Practical Conscious Creation Tip No. 53

Passionate Production

The most important ingredient in a successful work life is passion. First, try to find or create a job/business that fills you with passion overall—
—Whether that is because of what you are doing
—How you are doing it
—Who you are doing it for.

If you are in a role that isn't completely satisfying, at least try to find some major aspect of it that brings you joy. For example:
—You may not be crazy about the boss, but you love the product you are marketing;
—You are thrilled that you are not being tied to a desk for eight hours a day;
—You really love your co-workers and enjoy being part of a team;
—Your job allows you to be very creative;
—You get to travel to exciting cities and exotic places;
—Your company pays for the education that will enable you to achieve a better job in the future.

If you cannot generate any degree of passion for what you are doing, first examine if this reflects how you are living the rest of your life (i.e. not satisfied with anything and thus requiring a hard look at yourself)—or if it really is just the job. If it's just the job—whether it's one where you work for someone else or work for yourself—then you need to change it. Energy and prosperity will flow abundantly where you are feeling passionate and happy.

Conscious Creation in the Workplace

How often do you find yourself wishing your work environment was better, that your boss was more respectful, that your colleagues weren't so cliquish or irresponsible, or that the people you supervise were more committed and responsive to your direction? Do you sometimes think about quitting and moving on?

Before you do that, why not use your Conscious Creation skills to seek improvement in the situation? Take the initiative first!

When transforming the workplace, the first thing you must do is look at what you are emitting. If you are allowing your anger, frustration, and anxiety to dominate your presence, then you are contributing to the environment you are experiencing. Once you neutralize the negativity factor, by choosing instead to vibrate in the high range, you will start to see a change. Never go into work dreading the day, anticipating problems, or feeling overwhelmed at the workload on your desk. This energy will set the tone for what you receive that day. Make sure you start your day with a positive, optimistic, and joyful attitude of exuberance. Think to yourself: "What great adventure or wonderful experience will I have today?"

Now that you've started shifting your behavior, let's look at what you can do to reshape your environment. Consider the following five scenarios:

Your Boss, Clients, and Others Higher on the Food Chain

If you are feeling disrespected, unappreciated, or unacknowledged, then there are several actions you can undertake. The first is to act toward your supervisors the way you wish to be treated. Show them great respect, wonderful appreciation, and acknowledgment for what they do for you. Let the positive energy flow from you first. You brighten their day, since the s--t flows downhill and they are feeling the pressure, too.

Secondly, begin to visualize—with the emotional component—the type of interactions you want to have, the specific acts of regard and respect that you would like to see offered to you. Feel lifted, respected, recognized, and happy since you've been spoken to with encouragement instead of commanded to do something.

If you anticipate that there is a matter ahead that could be unpleasant or you're interacting with someone who often mistreats you, start by putting yourself in a cocoon of love. Allow that love to permeate every cell in your body. This is your transformative armor.

Now, before you meet, cast your "love net" over that person. See him or her transformed with love, compassion, regard, and kindness. Then project movies in your mind of all the great things that will occur in your meeting and the type of positive interactions you seek. Allow your high-frequency energy to set the tone. You can use this technique with any of the people you encounter professionally.

Group Dynamics

The first and foremost action you can take is to walk into a meeting with a genuine smile and your welcoming warmth. This should immediately have some effect on the low-vibration people in the room! Make sure that all of your comments are issued from a high-vibration space—you can discuss potential downsides, but do it in a constructive way. Monitor your words to ensure that whatever you are contributing raises the frequency in the room. If you are the leader, then you may want to see if you can begin the meeting by asking everyone what they would like to achieve and then formulate a short image or "guided meditation" of what you'd like to accomplish given everyone's input. That Consciously Creates a positive intention for the resolution and achievement of outcome.

Co-workers

Every company has its gossips, people who blame others, individuals who fail to pull their weight, and so on. The first thing to remember is that you are responsible for how you respond or react—and you actually don't need to do either. You can simply stay in your high-frequency state and not allow others to make you angry, annoyed, or disgusted. Focus on your own path, responsibility, and personal satisfaction.

However, if their work impacts yours, then you should use your power of positive vibration and visualization to start changing the dynamic. Once you've done that, use a strategy of high-vibration, positive word-choice communication to propose new solutions to your interactions. Meditate and ask for guidance on what and how you should suggest those new solutions. You'll receive great answers as long as you are vibrating with positive intentions!

People You Supervise

Lead by example. Use your high-vibration attitude and communications as a bellwether for your staff. Make your team members conscious of their own vibrations. Set up contests to eliminate negative communications. Reward those who make the most progress and show the most regard for others. Or simply compliment those who demonstrate high-vibration leadership. Encourage your staff to set their own intentions for their achievements and their behaviors, using Conscious Creation and visualization.

When you have staff whose work or actions need guidance, direction, or correction, first cast your love net, set an intention for a positive result, visualize what you want to see happen (with emotion—i.e. see yourself enthusiastically congratulating that person for making the change) and then begin the dialogue with high-frequency communication techniques.

Physical Environment

Some of the problems that cause dissonance are space limitations, lack of windows or uplifting light, and dingy or unkempt upkeep.

With space limitations, create a radiance around you that you feel extends well beyond your cubicle or desk. Let your positive vibration energy extend outward. Open your space to a feeling of expansion, knowing that your support and freedom comes from the entire reaches of the Universe, not just your little office space and immediately adjacent co-workers. Make your space your own. Bring joyful items or put fun screen savers on your computer. Let your personality shine! Own your space with loving energy!

With the issue of limited natural light, make sure you leave the building at least once every day to get that wonderful "hit" of natural energy from the outdoors and sun, then bring your sunshine back into your space. If you can have a say in the illumination, install or ask your employers to install full-spectrum lighting because this elevates vibration and mood. Allow yourself to do a short meditation when you feel the need for it so you can replenish your "light from inside."

Now when it comes to the upkeep of the office, you can choose not to leave it to your bosses if they have neglected the situation. You can be the force for upliftment for everyone in the office! Volunteer to head up a crew on a Friday to clean files, repaint the office, create order—whatever will create pride and positive energy in the office. Ask the boss to pay for lunch for everyone who

Practical Conscious Creation Tip No. 54

Go With the Work Flow

You will often find that you've scripted a meeting, a project, or a program in your head that doesn't turn out exactly as you planned or envisioned. You can waste a lot of energy trying to force your program back the direction you want it to go, or you can go with the work flow and see where the energy is taking you. Open yourself to new solutions. Listen to your higher power's gentle redirection that perhaps there is something better in store—or a new pathway for you to follow.

participates, and encourage your boss to join the crew. Turn it into a fun project to which everyone plans and contributes. Let it be a team-building venture. With your cleanup effort, set a group intention to open up a stream of positive energy that allows goodwill to flow and greater success and prosperity for the whole company.

Employ your wonderful abilities in Conscious Creation in the workplace and you will see a transformation in yourself and everyone around you!

Unearth and Unleash Your Hidden Entrepreneur

I'll bet you didn't know that you were really an entrepreneur in denial. You've just been afraid to come out of the closet. You've been too terrified of taking that leap. But it's there—whispering in your ear. *What if I just worked for myself? What if I could just make money without going to a 9 to 5 job? What if I could just do something I love and get paid for it?*

Then that other ego and fear-driven voice kicks in: *But what would I do that I'd be any good at that people would pay me for? How can I know that I could really pay the bills? How do I dare let go of security when I have to support my family or pay the mortgage? How do I know I wouldn't make a mess of things if I'm on my own?*

Well today's economy might have just "out-ed" you. You may have little choice but to get out of your security zone and start looking for new alternatives. Even if you haven't lost your job, you may just need to start earning some money from new sources to augment dwindling reserves.

While you may not be a "natural" entrepreneur like I am—a serial entrepreneur who has only worked for others for four of my nearly 60 years—if you have the passion, the creativity, the committed work ethic (note I didn't say hard work, just commitment to work!), and the faith that the Universe will assist you, then you can do it, too. And you can be successful at it. So let's look at those four factors individually.

Passion

What do you love? What burns in you and ignites your dreams? Entrepreneurs start businesses for two reasons—they want to do something that they love or know well, or they see a void in the marketplace, something they can offer that is in demand (we'll address this more in creativity). But the entrepreneurs who succeed most quickly and at the highest levels are those who are in love with what they are doing. That passion can take several different forms:

- A hobby or professional pursuit that engages them and their interest
- A love for serving others and helping those people be happier or more successful
- A general love for people and working with others
- A passion for the process, the kind of work they are doing
- A joy for simply being on one's own and not taking direction from others
- A knowledge that he or she has a better way or a better widget, and there are people just waiting for it to help make their lives or jobs better

So ask yourself: Where does your passion lie?

Creativity

A successful entrepreneur always finds a way to be distinctive in the business world. This is called your Unique Selling Proposition (USP).

For example, you can be a real estate agent just like a lot of other real estate agents, but you can creatively set yourself apart in many different ways—the way you market yourself, the kinds of properties in which you specialize, a special gift you give your buyers and sellers, a unique service you provide that others don't, a certain market you serve, and so on.

If you are selling a product, your USP might be that your product is different from anything on the market, or you package it differently, or sell it bundled with other products. What product can you offer that is unique?

If it's a service business, perhaps you offer a service not available in your area. You create a service that few are doing and that serves a distinctive niche. Or you do it better than the competitors and can prove it.

Your product or service doesn't have to be completely different from what is already in the market—it just has to *appear* to be different by virtue of how you position it in your marketing. And then it will resonate with those people who need it or who are perfectly attuned to what and how you are offering it.

For example, there are many other people in the spiritual, self-help genre that address manifesting as their core value, but they are not me! They don't build their premise around *Practical Conscious Creation* and the fact that you can actually create a blueprint, and then make it happen by anchoring Conscious Creation practices into every aspect of your daily life. That's my USP.

So get creative. What can you offer, create, serve, or position that is unique to you? What market can you serve that is now underserved?

Work Ethic

Yes, entrepreneurialism takes work. And sometimes it can be more than 9 to 5. But it's not necessarily hard work. When you are doing what you love and embarking on something of your very own, it can be easy work, because the doors will just begin to open. However, if you go into it tentatively, half-heartedly, or fearfully, then the Universe can't support you. Give it your heart even if you don't have much money. When you show the Universe you are committed and willing to work, then you will find answers to your challenges, people to help you, customers to buy your product or service, and money that will begin to flow your way.

So what kind of a commitment are you ready to make? This doesn't mean that you have to quit your day job immediately to start your new venture, perhaps it's something you start on the side and grow. But whatever it is, nurture it fully and completely so that it will eventually sustain you.

Faith in the Universe

This element is often overlooked in the harsh light of the business world. Even if you don't initially have faith in yourself, if you have faith in the Universe to support you, then you will begin to succeed. If you are living in confidence that the Universe has your best interests at heart, and you are open to its gentle guidance, then your business will thrive.

The opposite of faith is fear, and the need for control. Yes, you need to have a plan and be firmly acting on that plan, but feeling desperate to maintain "control" is just another way of expressing the fear that you are on your own and that no one or no force is there to help you.

Let go and trust. Surrender to the Universe. Have faith in the Source Power to be your co-pilot in your new venture. If you have trust, all the answers to your questions and challenges will come forth easily and quickly, and you will be guided to take the actions that will be right for your growth and maturity as a business person.

Practical Conscious Creation Tip No. 55

Minding Your Masterminding

If you feel alone in your personal or business life, and you really would like to have a support group of like-minded people, try putting together a Mastermind group. And it is even better if they are Conscious Creators—individuals who understand the power of personal empowerment, self-determination, and self-responsibility. Look around your social and professional circles for people whom you trust and for whom you have regard. Don't be intimidated if your prospective mastermind partners are folks with more experience than you, or whom you perceive to be more successful. Those are just the kind of people you want to connect with—people who can provide guidance and help you advance. You're looking for compassionate individuals who are willing to share what they've learned and are team players; they like to support others. The goal of the group is to provide assistance, guidance, and information for each other. If everyone is on the same page, it should be a synergistic process—each person grows and benefits from the process and the group evolves as well. In a Mastermind group, you can decide the ground rules together. You can discuss your personal struggles, your business challenges, or your spiritual evolution—whichever format the group decides upon. Inaugurate your group effort with a positive visualization of what you want it to be!

So, how can you expand and practice your faith in the Universe? Start by trusting your intuition and the messages you are receiving. Then remember that everything happens for a reason and allow yourself to be redirected if you are gently nudged in a new direction. Keep your eye on your goal and don't be fixated on how you get there. The Universe may have other great ways to ultimately get you to your desired success.

An entrepreneur with these four traits—passion, creativity, willingness to work, and faith—is nearly unstoppable. These are the bedrock values of a successful entrepreneur. Certainly knowledge of the market, financial resources, marketing savvy, and other business tools are valuable and can increase the rate of success, but you must first have these four core values to create a satisfying and successful entrepreneurial venture. Start by finding, instilling, and cultivating these values in your work life—and you'll be on your way.

Oops! Was that you peeking out of the entrepreneurial closet?

Practical Conscious Creation Tip No. 56

Walking Conscious Creation

While sitting quietly and meditating are the traditional ways to get into the Conscious Creation mode, I find that walking is also a very conducive way to start the energy flowing. One reason is that you are outside in nature, deeply breathing fresh air already! Your body is getting energized just by your movement. You feel good because you are doing something nice for your health. What a perfect setting for Conscious Creation—you're already flowing positive energy! So why not direct your thoughts inward to your heart? Find what you most want to manifest. And start visualizing while you walk, feeling great about your vision, that every positive step takes you closer to your dream! Just make sure that while you are visualizing, you don't walk into a fire hydrant or tree!

Chapter 11

Health

You don't have to wait till January to create a clean bill of health. That, of course, is the time when people who overdose on the excess of the holidays are trying to make amends for their indulgence. It's also the time of the year when people make New Year's resolutions. Many of those have to do with getting into shape, changing and monitoring eating habits, eliminating unhealthful activities like smoking, setting weight goals, and establishing an exercise routine. Those intentions are all wonderful and should be applauded. The hope is that people who set such intentions actually follow through and stay vigilant in practicing them.

Start with a Clean Bill of Health

But no need to wait until January when you can start impacting your health today! And not just by starting a great fitness regimen and going to the gym three times a week, or by cutting portions and choosing the right foods.

Health is also about managing your energy and clearing the energy blocks that cause dis-ease. Our illnesses are a result of emotional energetic charges plugging the free flow of our frequency and vibrational waves through our energy pathways. When the flow gets stopped up, your body begins to stagnate in that location, eventually reflecting physically what is happening in the "energy body"—that charged field of particles that surrounds you and permeates your physical being. When emotions—or memories that create strong fearful or painful emotions—lodge themselves in your energetic and physical body, they fester, creating aches, pains, and sickness. So essentially every tumor or other illness begins somewhere in your energy system first, then works its way into a physical reality within your body.

So what does this mean? Undoubtedly you have heard of miracle cures by healers or people having their diagnosed diseases just evaporate. The reason is that these individuals began clearing such blocks on a deep level, and correspondingly their physical abnormality disappeared.

But it also means that you have tremendous power over your future health and an ability to begin changing the current state of your health. Becoming healthy or staying healthy requires your diligence at rooting out emotional blockages and keeping your pathways clear.

Here are some of the ways you can help that process along:

- **Clear negative energy blocks.** Get into a quiet or meditational mode. Once you've calmed your mind and gone inside, begin surveying your body. Where do you feel blockages, pain, or illness? Is there anything you can intuitively tell is connected to each problem or discomfort? Ask your body questions: *What is this about? Is there a message to be learned here? What do I need to release? What am I holding onto that is no longer serving me?* Stay quiet and listen for the answers. Then once you've received your answers, begin setting intentions to let go of those energy blocks. Create affirmations that support the release of those obstructions. Do the work to clear fear, regret, disappointment, and anger surrounding specific experiences, beliefs, and memories that are inhibiting your health. Release the negative vibrations that are clogging up your system. The bonus benefit is that when you start raising your frequency, you'll also be a better and faster manifestor!

- **Reexperience your memories.** Some of those memories are doing you harm, lodged in your body with the pain that you shoved down inside when they occurred. (That's why a deep massage can sometimes cause someone to remember a hurtful old memory, resulting in sudden sadness and tears.) Allow those memories to resurface, and reexamine them. Feel again the original pain. Live through that pain, and don't rebury it. Experience it. Cry. Let the emotion out of the box and it will finally be free to go. So will your pain.

- **Refresh your chakras.** Clear and refresh your seven chakras on a regular basis, making sure they are spinning in the right direction and without obstruction. Many books on auras and chakras have suggestions on ways to do this, but generally the easiest is to listen to a guided meditation backed by beautiful music. It's a relaxing and soothing way to direct your intention through specific exercises that cleanse your vortexes.

- **Consider Reiki or Reconnective Healing.** Reiki is a type of energy work that enables the Reiki practioner or Reiki Master to direct universal healing energy into the places where you are blocked. This can be very effective for some people in eliminating pain and helping to resolve illness. Reconnective Healing Practitioners serve as catalysts for a new bandwidth of light, energy and information to correct physical, mental and emotional inbalances in the body, oftentimes resulting in instantaneous cures or recoveries.

- **Be attuned to your body.** Your body will tell you when you are tense, fearful, angry, unsettled, or worried. Listen for the signs of discomfort, then probe your mind and body to discover what emotion/feeling/belief is not in alignment with ease and flow. Once you've gotten deeply in touch with your inner self, begin the process of releasing. Set intentions, meditate, breathe, change your thoughts/change your vibration, call down golden light to cleanse and illuminate your body and let go of whatever is causing dis-ease. You can also exercise to enhance peace of mind, listen to relaxing or inspiring music, or perhaps join a spiritual group with a philosophy that emphasizes inner knowledge and self-healing.

- **Speak your truth.** Don't repress your feelings. Be honest with people, but be diplomatic. Speak your authentic truth. Express yourself in a positive way, but resolve what is eating at you. If you can't confront the person, write a letter. And if it's really something you cannot broach directly, write a letter but don't send it—just store it or burn it. Expel the poison from your body.

- **Seek the aid of an intuitive healer or counselor.** There are times when your emotions and beliefs are so deeply rooted that you will have trouble getting to them. Some of these feelings may in fact be holdovers from previous lives. If you have confidence in a particular intuitive counselor or your friends have had experiences with someone they trust, you may want to consider this alternative. A good spiritual counselor or healer will be able to discern where these blocks are and may assist or guide you in clearing them from this life or previous ones.

So can you effect an instant miracle cure? Perhaps. However, if not, you may see improvement over time. Adapting these techniques will prevent more illness in the future. Should you forego seeing a doctor? No. Please continue to pursue whatever allopathic medical care that is recommended, but at least use these complimentary healthcare strategies alongside mainstream ones. And if possible, try to find a doctor who understands the power of vibrational medicine and human energy.

In summary, you have the opportunity to create a clean bill of health at any time. Remember that this is also the time to attend to your energy body, not just your physical body.

Getting Healthy The Fun Way: Twelve Tips for Healing and Getting Fit Joyfully

For most of us, getting healthy is a chore. We have to drag ourselves to the gym, swallow a gazillion vitamins, go to the physician's office, and sit around for hours before being seen by the doctor, and then follow through on the doctor's protocols.

The annoyance and resistance just makes us more energetically weak and slower to heal or grow fit.

Thus, in order to really tune up your body, you need to look at the healing and fitness process as fun! Shift your attitude into a state of welcome, enjoyment, confidence in what you are achieving, and plain old happiness! The more you are in a state of joy and love for the process, the faster your body will vibrate the energy to meet your mental images and gleeful emotional state. Set the tone and your body will follow!

So here are some ideas that you can implement that will speed your path to health.

1. Each day envision yourself as completely healed and in ideal physical shape. Create your vision, feel it, enjoy it, believe it. Know that your body is absolutely PERFECT! Do this without fail for 30 days, but try to make it part of your daily routine for the rest of your life.

2. When you take your vitamins, supplements, and any other medications, see them as bubbles filled with love going down your throat and then spreading all over your body, much like the bubbles children blow into the air. You're sending bubbles to your organs, muscles, tendons, and tissues to coat them with love! Personally, I just smile when I envision this image!

3. Dance a little every day with abandon and release the stress in a very positive way. Do this to the radio when you are getting dressed, do it in the shower to tunes in your head, do it when your favorite song comes on your iPod, dance in exercise class at the gym or when you are on the treadmill. My personal favorite is to dance in the pool to music.

4. Never go the doctor's or therapy without a great book, an iPod with your favorite music, or some other creative endeavor such as a sketch pad. Make the waiting time enjoyable.

5. Look forward to the doctor visit or therapy session. See such visits as your opportunity for a "tune-up." You're a Maserati that just needs a little tinkering to get you revving down the road again at 120 miles an hour. Or you're a Dolce & Gabbana gown that needs a bit of redesign to get ready for the next awards show appearance.

6. If you are confident in the doctor's recommendations, then follow his or her instructions. No point in going if you don't do what the doctor says. But don't make this a chore. Make it a gift to yourself—a gift of your health.

7. Explore alternative therapies. If you're into alternative therapies, I always look at these as wonderful ways to expand my world and my knowledge of energy. Personally, I use a wonderful mix of traditional but holistic practitioners and alternative healing specialists whose work is generally based in energy flow. I go eager to know more about how my body works and

Practical Conscious Creation Tip No. 57

Make Getting Fit a Family Affair

No need to feel isolated as you tune up your body. Together with your family members, create visions of how you all want to look and feel. Then develop a plan of action, deciding which activities you will undertake mutually to make your visions reality. By supporting each other as a unit, you are more likely to stay on track and reach your goals.

how I can manage my energy more efficiently. It's like going to college classes without paying tuition!

8. Don't drag yourself to the gym or workout! Go with zeal! Remember how you feel when it's over and envision the way you will look in your clothes. Post a reminder on your pop-up email calendar with an incentive, such as the favorite pair of pants you plan to buy when you get down to your ideal weight. Or play something catchy like the song YMCA on your cell phone ring tone to remind you to go! See your trip to the gym as a chance to make new friends or workout buddies. Going with friends is definitely a way to make working out more fun.

9. Find a yoga class. Yoga is so good for both the mind and the body. Search for a yoga studio close to home with classes that fit your schedule so there's no good excuse not to go.

10. Walk! Find a pretty place where you can stride for exercise and inhale the beauty. With the arrival of Daylight Savings Time, you can walk well into early evening after work, or even in the morning before you go. Pick your favorite iTunes. I have a special iPod file just with great walking music that makes me pick up the pace and puts me in a fantastic mood.

11. Get outdoors or try new exercises—hiking, bicycling, snowboarding, skiing, and so on. You already know that these are beneficial to you and fun, too. Get up from in front of the computer and go do more of them. And don't forget to try something new. I know several women who have lost weight and become devoted to bellydancing and hula hooping to music!

12. Lifestyle eating changes are often challenging, but look at them as a chance to expand your choices or learn new recipes. Go to the health food store and discover cool new prepared foods, new ingredients, and healthy new packaged goods. (I love some of the dairy-free ice creams, for example, and my regular grocery store makes a mean cashew-encrusted chicken ready to heat and eat!)

So give yourself a positive energy boost even before the endorphins kick in and you'll find yourself on the fast track toward greater health.

Practical Conscious Creation Tip No. 58

Look for Messages in Movies and TV

These days it's hard to go to the movies and *not* find a wonderful message about Conscious Creation and spiritual upliftment. If you are currently on this path, you will find plenty of support in the media now awakening to the concept of Conscious Creation and the critical value of choosing our thoughts. So today, if you want reinforcement for your beliefs and truths, turn off the news and scour the listings for something that will be more satisfying for your soul. You'll find an increasing number of these enlightened programs every day!

Chapter 12

Leisure Life and Personal Expression

Maybe you don't paint like the Great Masters or like Pablo Picasso, but do you have some form of artistic or soul expression?

Each human being is an artistic and creative expression of the Universe, of the divine and unlimited creative force. In order to be fully who we are, we must find a creative outlet. In order to fulfill our role as creative, ever-expanding beings on this planet, we are compelled to express ourselves in a form unique to our soul. When you are operating in this mode of creative expression, you will feel yourself fully alive, thriving, and happy. That is because you are tap-·ping that unlimited force that is coming through you.

So it behooves each of us to find one or more ways for our creativity to express itself outside of the workplace. Creativity within work is also a wonderful form of expression, but it is not the same thing. You may also not think of some of your activities as artistic, because they are commonplace functions, but if you do them with flair, you may indeed be expressing your artistic self.

True Artistry/Soul Expression

Let's look at ways that you can release your unbounded creative spirit. While you may already be doing some of these things, there may be other ideas here that you can add to your creative portfolio:

- **Music, Song, and Dance:** Learn to play an instrument with instruction or teach yourself to play using music on your iPod. Join a band or local orchestra. Record music digitally and edit it on your computer. Create specialty playlists of others' works. Sing alone or sing with groups. Do karaoke. Take singing lessons. Take ballet lessons. Join an ethnic dance group. Take a ballroom dancing course. Compete in dance contests. Dance for fun at home where nobody sees you. Create your own dance and put it on YouTube.

- **Performing:** Take up acting or attend acting classes. Perform in local theatre. Create a one man/woman show. Read books aloud to an audience. Sing with a choir, band, troupe, or other group. Do a musical showcase at a nightclub. Try stand-up comedy. Perform with a dance group. Stage your own dance showcase. Invite people to a concert you host or promote. Orchestrate a musical review.

- **Painting, Sketching, Sculpting, Paper Sculpting/Origami:** Take formal art instruction, or just start putting images to canvas or paper. Explore various media—oil, pencil, acrylics, charcoal, and so on. Paper sculpting and origami provide plenty of creative expression. Explore sculpting in metal, wood, stone, or other material.

- **Writing:** If you've always had an urge to write—to express yourself through the written word—start putting pen to paper (or perhaps laptop or tablet if you prefer). There are more avenues than ever. You can now blog, tweet on Twitter, create newsletters, or write books, plays, short stories, magazine articles, or poetry.

- **Home Decorating:** Many people find their self-expression in their homes. Looking for or creating the perfect decorative elements in a home or vacation getaway can be very artistically rewarding.

- **Home Crafts:** Men and women can both find terrific self-expression through traditional crafts undertaken in their leisure time at home. Some of these might include: furniture making, antique refinishing, needlecraft, scrapbooking, quilting, woven crafts, folk crafts, greeting cards, and more.

- **Fashion Design and Creation:** Fashion is a passion for many people. Girls especially get charged up about designing perfect outfits from both store-bought and self-created clothing, and this love of fashion often carries into adulthood. Some ways to indulge the fashion passion include creative design, sewing, accessory making, hat creation, appliqués, sparkle application, t-shirt decorating, and so on.

- **Jewelry, Design, and Creation:** Jewelry design and creation is a wonderful way to show off works of your own making. Consider gemstone cutting, cabochon making, jewelry design, silver or goldsmithing, beading, and more.

- **Photography:** Using today's digital cameras, photography can be an easy and artistic hobby. Furthermore, digital technology and websites that offer places to show, archive, and sell photos to friends and the public are making it easier for a photographic artist to get a feeling of immediate recognition.

- **Gardening and Floral Design:** Growing a handsome and well-tended garden is an art in itself. Cultivating beautiful flowers for cutting and arranging is highly rewarding, and there are many flower arranging classes available in most communities. Don't overlook the joy of growing vegetables and eating your own produce!

- **Collecting, Model Building, and Displaying:** Collecting in itself may be rewarding, but there is tremendous artistry in assembling a great collection, enhancing it, then displaying it. While the different types of items people can collect is uncountable, here are just a few of the more traditional ones: trains, dolls and dollhouses, toys, model cars, model aircraft, kites, minerals, coins, stamps, cottages/villages, holiday decorations, and animal collections, carvings, and paintings. Don't let yourself be limited to the traditional. Find whatever intrigues you and collect it! No matter how wacky some people might think it is!

- **Parenting:** While parenting in itself can be very creative, many men and women find their artistic expression in activities they do with or create for their children: birthday parties, tree houses, room decor, excursion planning, storytelling, and so on.

- **Holiday Decorating and Party Planning:** If you were one of those kids who loved dressing up in elaborate costumes for Halloween, chances are you might get a big charge out of doing a first-rate scary display at your house as an adult, finding all the right ghouls, goblins, and gravestones. Many people love decorating for the holidays, whether that's Halloween, Thanksgiving, Christmas, Hannukah, Fourth of July, or a birthday party. Pick a theme and have fun!

- **Pottery, Ceramics, and Glassmaking:** Molding a piece of art with your hands and your talents is a great form of expression. Consider pottery, ceramics, or even glass making or blowing, mosaic design, tile making or tile painting, and so on.

- **Automotive:** Refurbishing antique automobiles and motorcycles, and painting them in glistening colors, bright brass, shiny chrome, or searing flames is an excellent way for men to let out their inner artist.

- **Cooking, Baking, Winemaking, Beer Brewing, and Entertaining:** People of both genders find great satisfaction in creating great works of art in the kitchen and in dining table décor. There is considerable artistry in cooking, food presentation, baking, winemaking, and beer brewing.

- **Pet Life and Pet Habitat:** So you love your pet? Here's another great way to be creative. Dress up your dog. Design the perfect doghouse. Make dog pillows. Craft the perfect cat scratching post. Formulate the ideal aquarium. Or build a fun habitat for a small animal or bird.

- **Join a Festival Planning Crew:** Very few things are more creative and fun than a themed festival—whether it's a renaissance festival, an ethnic clan gathering, a harvest fair, a country and western music event, a food festival, and so on. Find one you resonate with, and join the group staging it. Make your costume and start building the booths and planning the plays. You will have great creative fun.

- **Sports and Competitive Events:** Some sports are very creative by virtue of what their followers bring to them. For example, I know few people as creative as balloon pilots, who put a great deal of expressive effort into designing their balloons, naming them, getting the crew jackets just right, and generating many fun ways to establish their identity in the ballooning community and at balloon rallies or races. Sailboat enthusiasts and vintage car racers share many of the same creative instincts.

Allow yourself to Consciously Create the opportunity to creatively express yourself. If you set the intention, you will find a path that will lead you to your ultimate soul expression.

How Pets Help You Grow

Having a pet is one of the most rewarding opportunities for personal growth. Pets teach you unconditional love. They are a daily reminder of the power of unlimited love and complete trust. A pet expands your heart every time you look at it though the eyes of love, touch it/hold it, and watch with pride as it learns and grows. If you are having difficulty knocking down the walls around your heart, start with loving an animal first and then extend your loving energy to begin embracing your human counterparts.

Pets also teach you patience. No one who has house-trained an animal would ever doubt that! It takes time and patience to coax a pet into behaviors that conform to your lifestyle. It takes patience to nurse an ill pet back to health. It takes more patience when an animal is misbehaving or excited, and you must contain or redirect its attention. As you grow your patience with your beloved pet, you will learn patience for everything else in your life to manifest in due time.

Pets bring out your playfulness. As an adult with numerous commitments and responsibilities, there are few opportunities to really nurture that wonderful child inside of you. With a pet, you can indulge your inner child all the time. Whether it's chasing Frisbees with your dog, teasing a kitten with a ball of yarn, bounding after your bunny, teaching your parrot to talk, or taking a leisurely stroll with your horse, your playfulness comes to the fore. In these instants when you are fully present to play, you are living in the moment.

Pets teach you self-discipline. You cannot have and love a pet without caring for it when it needs attention. You must feed it on schedule, you may need to walk it, you have to clean up after it, and you must buy food and pet supplies before they run out. From this you must learn to give yourself as much commitment to self-care as you do your pet.

Practical Conscious Creation Tip No. 59

Going to Places of Sacredness and Worship

Much of the time today our Conscious Creation and Universal Connection is done in private within our own homes or perhaps in nature. But once in a while it's great to bridge that spiritual connection in a place where others also share a sense of sacredness. This can offer a special recharge to your own spiritual practice. So if it resonates with you, consider paying a visit to a local spiritual shrine, an ashram, a temple, a church if its aligned with your philosophy (Unity and Science of Mind share many of the Conscious Creation principles), a noted sacred site or energy-positive community such as Sedona, Arizona; Mount Lassen, California; or Ashville, North Carolina. Find a place where you are comfortable and soak up the positive energy to reinvigorate your own. If you travel internationally, perhaps you would like to explore one of the locations that are renowned for their positive vortex of spiritual energy, including the Pyramids in Egypt, Stonehenge in England, and Mount Olympus, Greece. Martin Gray's *Sacred Earth* and Christop Engels' *1000 Sacred Places:The World's Most Extraordinary Spiritual Sites* are both excellent starting places to plan your trip.

Pets can help you engage in the world. Dog lovers especially have wonderful opportunities for connection. There are chances to meet people in dog parks and dog affinity organizations, opportunities to convene with other dog lovers at dog training programs, the ability to participate in dog shows and dog performance events, train your dog to be a therapy dog for hospital visits, or participate in the training of guide dogs and service dogs. There are online communities for all types of pet owners and pet lovers. Most pets love to party! Let them be an inspiration for you to get out into the world and meet new like-minded pet lovers.

Pets teach you compassion. There are times when you will want to exercise compassion for a pet who is having a difficult time or is suffering from illness or injury. Your empathy, kindness, and love increase your ability to be compassionate with others as your heart opens.

Pets help you to be a Conscious Creator because they keep you positive, upbeat, loving, and in a state of happiness—all vital aspects for living a high-frequency life.

So if you've been looking for ways to be more in alignment with the Universe, you may want to make a visit to your local animal shelter to adopt a sweet, new family member who barks, meows, or chirps!

Growing a Conscious Creation Garden

Would you like to see the power of love and Conscious Creation at work? Then you might want to plant or tend a garden or grow your own vegetables. Plants feel your love and respond to touch. Even more amazing, they sense your emotions and respond to your encouraging thoughts. Don't believe me? Pick up a copy of the astounding book *The Secret Life of Plants* by Peter Tompkins and Christopher Bird. The subtitle of the book says it all: "A Fascinating Account of the Physical, Emotional, and Spiritual Relations Between Plants and Man." Indeed it is!

While I was researching my first book, *The Art of Conscious Creation: How You Can Transform the World*, I was lucky enough to read *The Secret Life of Plants* and other books that describe studies illuminating this connection between species. Two of my favorite studies are the following:

- A scientist hooked monitors to the plants of a woman who had a terrible fear of flying and documented her plants' response to the exact moment she took off on a flight 3,000 miles away.

- A husband/wife team of scientists split their students into two teams. Each team was assigned the task to plant and nurture a group of identical seedlings. One team was quietly taken to the side and told their seedlings had been "irradiated" and would sprout faster. Thus, both sets of students set to work and—lo and behold—the "irradiated" seed did grow larger faster. However, the truth was soon revealed. The husband and wife scientists had done nothing out of the ordinary to those seedlings. The reason they grew so effectively was the students' belief that they had special seedlings. The plants were responding to their intention and belief.

There have also been numerous studies showing that plants respond well to inspiring and peaceful music, and tender ministrations. If you love a plant, it will most likely thrive!

So if you are seeking wonderful ways to practice your Conscious Creation skills, why not do it in the garden? Take loving care of your plants. Talk to them. Sing to them. Play music for them. Envision their blossoms, their rich greenery, and their healthy growth. Plant vegetables and tend them with joy. Make sure you are in a positive, upbeat mood when you handle them or you will inculcate your negative energy into them. Maybe you can even offer your high-frequency produce at a local farmer's market!

So take your gardening seriously, even if it's just for fun! If you have roses, learn how to cut them so that they spring right back with more blossoms. Look for organic plant food and insect-resistant fertilizers for your plants. You may want to attend gardening and vegetable growing classes, or flower arranging courses.

If you're seeking a way to invest your care and attention in something that will yield a beautiful and delicious harvest—a tangible feedback for your efforts—then grab your trowel and start planting!

Practical Conscious Creation Tip No. 60

Journaling for Fun and Growth

Remember when you kept a diary as a pre-teen or teen and you recorded all your deepest thoughts? Those may have been the ramblings of a child, but today adults are finding true therapeutic and spiritual value in journaling their thoughts. Journaling is a beneficial and effective tool that allows you to get in touch with your heart, your soul, and the Universe. People report astonishing break-throughs in clarity, consciousness, and Conscious Creation by writing down what they feel, what they think, and what they learn through their open channel from the Source. This is the place to pour out your pain to release it, to forgive others and to create your dreams. If you wish put some of your leisure time toward this practice, I encourage you to pick up and explore these two books: *Writing Down Your Soul: How to Activate and Listen to the Extraordinary Voice Within* by Janet Conner or *Journalution: Journaling to Awaken Your Inner Voice, Heal Your Life and Manifest Your Dreams* by Sandy Grason.

Service: The Extraordinary Gift of Self

There are few acts that have greater repercussions in the world than committing yourself to enhancing the welfare of another. Service to an individual, cause, or humanity as a whole is one of the most generous and rewarding uses of your leisure time. The enduring gift of service is that it blesses both the giver and the receiver.

As you parse out where you choose to spend your non-encumbered hours, consider earmarking time every week or every month for selfless service in support of others. There are so many ways that you can make a difference. Know that you are creating waves of positive high-frequency vibrations for yourself and for those whom you aid—whether you are in direct or indirect contact with the ultimate beneficiaries.

Here are some of the ways you might be of service:

- Volunteer as a Big Brother or Big Sister.
- Seek out and join Conscious Cause organizations that take a stand on behalf of the voiceless, the planet, animals, key issues, and the betterment of humankind.
- Support nonprofit organizations that seek cures and improve the health of those afflicted by disease.
- Join a faith-based or spiritual center's community outreach program.
- Participate in a literacy program, or teach your skills to those who can benefit.
- Join organizations that support military men and women and their families.
- Get active in a group that aids the elderly in your community.
- Help raise scholarship money for needy students.
- Volunteer as a coach for boys, girls, seniors, or the physically challenged.
- Participate in an organization that helps young men and women raise their self-esteem.
- Get involved in a community clean-up effort.
- Contribute your talents, gifts, foodstuffs, or crafts to a worthy organization.

Practical Conscious Creation Tip No. 61

Self-Help Lending Library

In today's economy, it's sometimes hard to justify spending a considerable amount of money on books, even if they are for your personal growth. So here are a couple of thoughts. If you haven't utilized the public library since you were in grade school, you'd be surprised at the depth of self-help offerings both in print and via audio recordings. So reactivate your library card!

Also, it is highly likely that many of your friends who are on the same personal growth path have dozens of books just sitting on their shelves. Get your friends together over dinner one night and agree to pool your self-help books into a group lending library. Either put them all at the same physical place where anyone can retrieve them fairly easily, hold a weekly book club to exchange books, or create a web page where people can see who has which book and then can swap them around the circle. Keep growing your circle and watch the books multiply. Happy reading!

- Find someone who needs help and mobilize the people and resources to provide assistance.

Bless others with your time, focus, and compassion—and you will be equally blessed!

Chapter 13

Holidays and Seasons

While the goal of this book is to make every day a Conscious Creation day, holidays lend themselves to a special celebration of the Conscious Creation arts. They provide the perfect time to stop and reflect on how we arrived at today and how we wish to move forward tomorrow.

Your B-Earth-Day

Sometime this year you will celebrate your birthday, or as one of my favorite notecards refers to it: "Your B-Earth-Day"—the day you arrived in physical form on this planet.

Some people bemoan this day as a reminder of years passing, aging bodies, achievements not fulfilled, and experiences not yet had. Others celebrate it with abandon and joy, an opportunity to celebrate their presence and aliveness, and a time to gather with friends and family to remember they are loved.

But somehow in either of these ways of marking a passing year, the sacredness is lost. It is often overlooked that you are a gift to the planet, and a gift to the soul of the solar system. Connected as you are through your spiritual self to the Universe, you are allowing the great Source energy to express itself and its expansion here on Earth. How wonderful to be a part of the great evolution of the Universe! You are a sacred being!

Our birthdays, then, should also be a time of reflection, a time of gratitude, and a time of reconnecting with the Universe. It's the perfect opportunity to honor that connection. And also to set intentions for the year ahead—to place our order, so to speak, for the changes we want to see in our lives and in ourselves.

So as your birthday approaches the next time around, plan ahead for a new kind of B-Earth-Day celebration—this one just between you and the Universe. Begin thinking about what it is that you want to contemplate on that day, jot it in a notebook, so that you can begin creating a special B-Earth-Day ritual that honors you in a truly spiritual way.

On the day of your remembrance—for that is what it truly is: an opportunity to connect with and remember who you really are—you will want to go to a beautiful and sacred place, either in your home or somewhere you can be alone outdoors, perhaps a spiritual shrine or under a tree in a quiet park.

First just connect with yourself. Breathe deeply for at least five minutes and relax. Open yourself to the flow of positive energy coming from above. See yourself connected to the Universe—the Source—by golden light flowing into the crown of your head. Let your mind release, relax into a state of peace, feel a warm glow of love in your heart for you, your higher self and for the Universe.

Now move into a state of gratitude. Reflect on all that you have achieved in your years and what you have that enriches your life today. Remember the people who have loved you and support you still. Think of all the fun and joy you have had in your life. Then begin to truly feel your gratitude for being allowed to be present in physical form, for the years on Earth that you have been granted, and for the wonders that have enabled you to be present today. Look back at all of this in awe, wonderment, amazement, and blessedness.

Now in this state of gratitude and connection, ask the Universe: *How can I live the best human experience in my next year? What should I know? What must I become? And what shall I do to live my best life in my next year, starting today with my B-Earth-Day?* Stay open to the answers. Listen now, but the answers may come immediately or much later. And just keep your mind focused on listening for at least 15 minutes. You may "hear" words in your mind, you may see images, you may just get a sense of knowing, or you may get a physical sense. Everyone receives information differently.

Once you have allowed yourself the opportunity to be in receptivity and reverence, then—and only then—you may offer the Universe a vision of how you would like the year to unfold, and what B-Earth-Day gifts you would like to have become reality. Remember to be living a high-vibration, positive life as part of your dream. View these images as already done, as if you are looking back from next year's B-Earth-Day. Remember to get into the emotion—the joy, gratitude, love, and excitement –of having just experienced such a blessed and wondrous year.

Conclude your special B-Earth-Day celebration with a blessing for yourself. Thank the Universe for who you are, for your spiritual connection, for your spiritual growth, and for how you have made the world a better place. Remember just how wonderful—and remarkable—you are. Thank the Universe for the gifts of human life and the everlasting lifetime of the spirit, and the light that you are on the planet.

February
President's Day: Leadership Honored

On President's Day we honor two of our greatest presidents, but I encourage you to take that day to expand your awareness toward honoring worthy leadership in general. It is a terrific time to be grateful for the leaders who are indeed strong in integrity, powerful in their commitment to right action, and imbued with the true spirit of love and grace.

What is it that you might be doing to support these good men and women who heft the weight of their communities on their shoulders—the ones for whom power is not a self-perpetuating goal, but a way to make the world a better place? Do you vote to elect and keep them in office? Do you volunteer in your community on programs they create? Do you offer your comments and input via mail or email? Do you send positive energy and white light to keep them healthy, protected, and strong? These are all great ways to keep building an inspired leadership for our cities, our states, and our country.

But do you ever think of yourself as a leader? Where do you exhibit leadership in your life? Do you just complain about the way things are, or do you takes steps to create change? Do you demonstrate leadership in the office, in your social community, at home, or with your family members? If you are not doing so now, could your leadership make a positive difference?

Make yourself a leader! Each of us can lead in ways that are gracious, collaborative, encouraging, spiritually uplifting, and powerfully inspiring. True leaders are not dictatorial; they are motivational. Look at how you can step into those shoes.

Here are some suggestions:

1. **Look at what skills you possess that create natural leadership.** What abilities do you have that lend themselves to a leadership role? Are you visionary, passionate, clear thinking, solution-driven, verbally communicative, persuasive, to name but a few?

2. **Where can you apply these skills to best use?** With co-workers and colleagues in your profession? Volunteering with community causes? Within your family unit of aging parents, brothers and sisters, other generations, and your immediate family? With friends who can be mobilized to do good works for others (for example, Habitat for Humanity)? At your

Practical Conscious Creation Tip No. 62

Valentine's Day: I Am LOVE!

As we enter February, in which Valentine's Day is such a symbol and reminder of romantic love, we are all reminded that love is the frequency that is the essence of the Universe. Each of us can be a powerful conduit for love in this dimension. We experience self-love; love for our family, the world, and other fellow Earth inhabitants; and spiritual/romantic love with an individual. Each of these paths of love connects us to the divine energy in unique and special ways. Each day I begin my day by getting in the universal flow and affirming to the Universe "I AM LOVE." It is amazing what this one statement does to change my outlook and ensure that I am in the right frame of mind before welcoming the rest of the world into my day. Each of us can use more love in our lives—and we can give more love. At the end of each day, ask yourself: "What have I done to increase love today—for myself, for my beloved, for my family, for the world?"

So let every beautifully rendered heart you see as Valentine's Day approaches remind you of your opportunity to fulfill your role as a loving presence on this planet.

school? In your Homeowner's Association? At your church or spiritual center of divinity? In local community organizations, city council, or community boards?

3. **Find a leadership void and fill it!** Lead not just because you want "to be a leader"; *lead because you have found something that matters to you*—and you can bring others together so that they can also lend their creative energy to its manifesting.

4. **Explore how you can become a more effective leader.** There are numerous books and CDs that illuminate the traits of effective leaders. You can hone your public speaking skills through the organization Toastmasters. You can find a mentor to coach you, or watch other leaders closely so you can emulate them. You can attend leadership conferences and seminars. You can ask for encouraging feedback from members of organizations you are already directing by asking: "How can I better serve and lead this group?"

5. **A leader's primary objective is to serve!** If you are reluctant to become a leader, remember that leading is really just *service*. You are helping others to bring out the best in themselves. And you are focusing the united energy of the group toward a positive change for the future.

So if on President's Day you are indeed already a leader, pat yourself on the back! If not and reading this inspires you to exert your leadership in the future, perhaps next year we will be toasting you on President's Day, too!

April
Watering Seedlings

Today is Earth Day! It is the time when we honor and re-dedicate ourselves to caring for our planet. And it is also spring when farmers and gardeners traditionally plant seeds in our glorious earth that will grow and ripen in the summer and fall.

But planting seeds is a metaphor for renewal—starting anew or creating something that never was before. And once you plant those seeds, you must water the seedlings and shower them with loving care. So this is an excellent time to look at your own life and decide which seeds you will plant for your future and the future of the planet, and how you will water, protect, and nurture them.

Practical Conscious Creation Tip No. 63

Time to Prune

The gardeners cut all 280 roses back in my garden this week. They look so barren—just a bunch of branches sticking up into the air. But I take great joy in knowing that this exercise in pruning will lead to an amazing renewal! In late March and early April here in California, my garden will be awash with fabulously gorgeous roses in every color of the rainbow (except white, since I'm addicted to color!). There will be solid color roses, blends, multi-colors, stripes, and reverses (a different color on each side of the petal). I can just imagine the smell and the feel of those soft petals, and the luscious bouquets adorning my desk and my home. Knowing that I will enjoy that beauty in the spring makes the winter much more enjoyable.

So my question is: what can you prune from your life now that will create rebirth, renewal, and brilliance in the near future? What habit or trait, what extra unnecessary task, can you eliminate that will burnish your life and make it the best year ever? Prune now and reap joy and inner peace as a benefit!

We can each waste our precious time looking back at what we did, what was done to us, and how we got where we are—continuing to let the past limit us. Or we can stop that indulgent behavior and instead put our energies toward planting positive new seeds that will ripen and enrich our lives in the years to come. So what is it going to be for you? Stunted growth or rampant growth?

Here are some of the areas where you can start planting and watering seeds:

- **Commit to educational enhancement.** Return to school, sign up for retraining programs, attend seminars, go for an advanced degree, subscribe to online courses.

- **Commit to professional evolution.** Evaluate if this is the right career path. If not, begin making plans and taking actions toward something that would bring you greater satisfaction—research new options, look for new opportunities, create your own job and pitch it to your current boss or a new company, start your own business, explore improving your resume and interviewing skills.

- **Commit to personal growth.** Buy books or ecourses, get a coach or mentor, join a coaching group that meets by phone, secure an accountability buddy, embark on a self-development program with a spouse or loved one, start a mastermind group.

- **Commit to relationship growth.** Go to counseling with your spouse or significant other, attend family counseling, carve out focused time for your relationship, listen to your partner with greater attention, take a course in couples communication, attend an anger management course, develop strategies to keep the romance alive. If you are single, join a singles activity group or sign up for an online dating program.

- **Commit to spiritual growth.** Join a spiritual community in your area, begin a personal spiritual practice of meditation and self-reflection, choose a spiritual mentor who will help you find your own path, sign up for a yoga program or other physically based spiritual practice, read books that can help you understand your relationship to the Divine.

- **Commit to become a better parent or better caregiver to your aging parents.** Practice more patience, learn new coping techniques, find new resources that provide assistance, align with others who have the background and experience to offer suggestions, and read magazines and books that open your eyes to new ideas.

- **Commit to greater self-care and self-love.** Get more exercise, eat better and healthier, pamper yourself, discover ways to honor and love yourself, work with experts to overcome low self-esteem and self-disregard, and practice affirmations and more conscious self-love and acceptance.

- **Commit to greater health management.** Take care of all the doctor/dentist appointments and annual screenings you tend to delay (mammogram, colonoscopy, and so on), get more exercise, eat better and healthier, find out what you're deficient in and take *all* your vitamins and supplements every day, continue looking until you find doctors or practitioners you like, explore alternative healthcare and modalities, and rest when you are not well instead of working through it.

- **Commit to greater fiscal management.** Reduce your credit card load, establish and keep to a budget, rectify your check book or get someone to do it for you, prepare your taxes in advance instead of the last minute, get professional help to resolve fiscal problems before they become legal and IRS dilemmas, negotiate payments with your creditors and keep to that payment schedule, and say NO when someone wants to go to the shopping mall (i.e. avoid temptation).

- **Commit to creating greater balance in your life.** Cut back on your work time, start a hobby that you've always wanted to try, spend more time at a hobby you love, commit time to be of service in the community, spend more time with family, take at least one vacation a year and some weekends away, carve out time for reading and relaxing, and schedule exercise time in your calendar so it doesn't slip away.

- **Commit to the planet.** Recycle more—not just paper—but plastics, batteries, and other results of man's production; use less energy and water; find ways to reduce your carbon footprint; choose earth-sensitive products; support earth-conscious corporations and causes; reduce paper waste, including contacting direct marketers to stop them from sending unwanted mailers and catalogues; refuse paper and plastic bags at stores; support organic growers; and grow your own vegetables and fruits.

These are just some of the possible seeds that you can choose to plant and water in your personal garden. Now is an excellent time to decide where you want to focus your attention so that your efforts will result in beautiful blooms and ripe results over the next year. So on our wonderful Earth Day, plant your seeds, pour a little water, and give those seeds a lot of your love! May you reap joy, love, prosperity, health and peace of mind when these seeds mature!

Practical Conscious Creation Tip No. 64

Daylight Savings Time is Back!

Even if there's snow on the ground where you live, Daylight Savings Time heralds the spring to come, but most of all it gives us one more hour in the day before we settle in for nighttime. So let's ask what we want to do with that extra time. More work? More chores? More errands? Why not use those extra hours deliciously for yourself? I love to walk in the two hours before dusk, that "golden light" time. But Daylight Savings Time also means I might be able to get in a half hour or more of meditation in the morning before I get to my desk, or perhaps in the evening in my backyard, amongst the trees, cooing doves, running waterfall, and fresh-smelling flowers. On the weekends, I can also spend more time outdoors reading wonderful mind/body/spirit books or perhaps immerse myself in a historical biography or novel. What can you do with those extra hours? How can you enrich your life, de-stress, find joy? Take a yoga class, visit friends who feed your soul, take your dog for a long walk, dance, sing, or indulge in a hobby that takes you away from the cares of the day, cart your kids to a culturally stimulating program that's interactive for adults, too, and so on.

Make a list of the things you wish to do and then block time for this in your calendar. And just to make sure you are creating the right energy for it, Consciously Create a visualization where you see yourself doing these things. Revel in the emotions of joy, relief, fun, ease, and satisfaction that go along with being in that experience. Now go enjoy those extra daylight hours!

July
Appreciating Our Freedoms

We all know that there is one incredible freedom that Americans celebrate on the Fourth of July each year and that is the freedom to live how we choose in our remarkable nation. For all of its faults, we often overlook how extraordinary it is, how our Founding Fathers sacrificed so much and were filled with such wisdom that has enabled our country to endure and thrive these 200+ years.

One way that we can experience this clearly is in our freedom to Consciously Create. There are very few nations in the world where one can conceive an idea and turn it into a successful enterprise just through vision and industriousness—especially if you are a woman. I often reflect on how grateful I am to live in the United States, where I dreamed of being a sportswriter, became one, then used that as a stepping stone for a nationally recognized career in media relations. Had I been born elsewhere—even in a country that only covertly oppresses women—the obstacles could have been staggering. And I am reminded of this each time I travel internationally and talk to women about their lives.

So let's put aside our reminders of economic strife, social inequities, urban decay, environmental crisis, eroding civil liberties, and other issues, and let's use the Fourth of July celebration to bless our nation and be thankful for its gifts. Then let's hold a vision of the next 200 years where we have fostered a nation that is truly a leader in peace, prosperity, equality, and sustainability. There's only one thing in our glorious Constitution today that my heart would like to see changed and that is the right of US citizens to bear arms. What a world we would inhabit if no one possessed guns! See the difference in Canada, where the homicide and violent crime rate is so drastically below our own. Yes! Let's keep envisioning an America where freedom also means the ability to go anywhere without fear!

We must treasure our freedom to live as we desire in the external world, but we should not forget how we live in our internal world. Are we free there as well? I will bet that you have forgotten many of the freedoms that you can give yourself, have given yourself, or may give yourself. Think for a moment and reflect on how free you feel inside? Are you free to enjoy the choices you make? Are you free to love yourself and to love others? Are you free to be radiant and happy? Are you free to think good thoughts and relax into them? Are you free

Practical Conscious Creation Tip No. 65

Time to Chill

In summer when everything just seems hot, we have a tendency to get irritated and short since we feel physically uncomfortable. So here's just a little reminder that chilling in our minds helps chill our bodies. Keep your cool when the temperature rises by feeling good, being in gratitude, being patient with yourself and others, and generally letting things flow. Imagine yourself a cool ocean wave, and just go with it! May you have many summer breezes to help you chill, too!

to enjoy your own company? Are you free to connect with people on a deep soul level? Are you free to pursue physical experiences that feed your inner self? Are you free to enrich your mind and heart with reading that uplifts and inspires you?

While you may often be aware of the sense of energetic restriction that makes you feel limited, claustrophobic, and disappointed—I certainly experience this sometimes—we forget that these are bindings that we have created. There is a world out there beckoning us to freedom. We have no boundaries. We are creatures born to freedom, with a birthright of *internal* freedom, as well as *external* freedom. So for today, be grateful for your freedom and truly begin to feel it! Let those straps, chains, bindings go—release them!—and let your inner freedom become your truth and your daily existence.

October
Halloween: The Real Haunts in Our Lives

At the time of ghouls, goblins, and ghosts, when scary fantasies take center stage, we need only look closely at our own inner thoughts to see scary fantasies that haunt our lives.

Each of us has created beliefs, memories, and fears that inhibit our unlimited capacity for Conscious Creation. Instead of soaring free in abundance, joy, and supreme health, we are caught in a web of our own making that keeps us earthbound and constricted. So how can you unbound these chains and create a magical life?

Here are some suggestions:

- **Remember that it's all in your head.** Most of your misery results from listening to the voices in your head. These are not real. You created them. Mostly they are about what you think you should be but aren't, or what someone else thinks of you, what you believe should be happening but isn't, or what you think someone else did to you. This is all fiction—scary, unreal stories. They aren't truth or reality. When these thoughts get out of control, banish them! You can live beautifully and happily by looking at reality instead of creating fiction.

- **Create an out-of-body experience.** Get out of your own head and look at

Practical Conscious Creation Tip No. 66

Drive, He Said

Summers are when people get in the car for long drives to see friends or go on vacation. Today, driving is often preferable to the headaches of air travel. So when you are driving on the road, consider *not* turning on the radio, CD player, or the iPod. Instead use this time to set new intentions and to refine your desires with clarity. While being careful not to "zone out" so that you are driving unconsciously, you can still use this valuable time for Conscious Creation. It's also a great opportunity to open your channel to receive and see what comes forth! Many of my best ideas present themselves while I'm driving!

yourself and the situation objectively. View yourself and the circumstances from the perspective of being someone else. What truth do you see that you wouldn't perceive through the filter of your own insecurities, beliefs, prejudices, and fears?

- **Stare down those goblins, mash those monsters, bust those ghosts.** Be courageous and simply tell those voices they don't count. Do not give them the power to make you unhappy and negative. If it's easier to do this by envisioning them as ghosts, goblins, and monsters, use that tool to dismiss and discharge them.

- **Put a spell on yourself.** Put a *happy* spell on yourself, and tell yourself that you will not let any of these negative thoughts break the spell. Live your life in the belief that all is well and everything will work out. Just ask for the guidance that will help resolve things in your highest good. Let the universal "spell" of *goodwill* be your intoxicant.

- **Choose heaven or hell.** Remember that your life is about choices. You can choose your own personal hell or you make choices that reach for heaven—decisions that are life-destructive or life-affirming. Deep down you know which is which, and you can resist those little devils who are whispering in your ear and luring you to the dark side.

- **Call on your archangels, water sprites, and fairies.** If you're going to believe in what you don't see, you might as well make it those beings who look after you and help to support you in positive ways. Ask for their support when you need strength, guidance, or additional aid in manifesting what you desire. You'll be surprised at how your unexpected support manifests!

So as Halloween approaches, just recall that it's a perfect time to rejoin the land of the living by letting go of the deadwood in your soul.

November
Thanksgiving Blessings: Gratitude Revisited

When the market declines and the economy dips, we tend to spiral down emotionally. We commiserate with friends and family about how bad things are and how tough we have it.

Thanksgiving comes along at a perfect time to count our blessings instead of our woes. Businesses send cards thanking their customers. Most people are grateful to share a repast with friends and family. Families say grace over the Thanksgiving meal. But gratitude should not be a once-in-a-while expression. It should be part of everyday living, a way of life.

Each of us is responsible for how his or her life unfolds. And if we are to pave the way for a successful and prosperous year ahead, Thanksgiving is the perfect time to shed a negative outlook and expression, and start projecting leadership, optimism, and faith.

If we live in gratitude, we:

- Enhance our direct connection with the Divine or the Universal Source that provides all;

- Increase our potential for and attraction of abundance;

- Improve the relationships we have with those around us;

- Give a blessing to whomever we show, demonstrate, or express our thanks;

- Feel better about receiving and accepting the gifts provided by the Universe;

- Raise our personal frequency and our ability to manifest faster;

- Raise the frequency of the planet.

It's up to you to be the one at the table that steers the conversation away from everyone's problems to topics that uplift, inspire, and excite. And you don't have to do this alone! Enlist other co-conspirators who will give you a wink of acknowledgement when they shift the conversation intentionally, too! So here are some suggestions on ways to truly embrace the spirit of Thanksgiving Day:

- Create a Thanksgiving scroll. Everyone in the family must write at least one thing for which they are grateful. Read these just before dinner commences.

- Do a special favor for someone in the family in gratitude for the many kindnesses they have shown you or deeds they have done on your behalf.

- Tell others in your family or dinner gathering what they mean to you and how they have blessed your life.

- Get together with others and go down to the local shelter to help serve dinner to the homeless.

- Call someone you know who could use a kind word and touch his or her heart with your voice. Or send a card.

- Share some of your abundance, joy, and inspiration with others—and maybe even a bit of your cooking!

- Make a deposit into a savings account, however small or large, as a show of thankfulness for the money that is coming your way.

- Create a list of alternative topics of conversation and present them to the family with a proposal that whenever the conversation starts to turn negative, someone introduces one of the chosen subjects—or another positive topic of their choosing. Make a humorous game of toasting whiners with wine!

- Look around the table and count your blessings—food, family, clothing, home, love, smiles, health, wisdom, and more. Focus on a vision of abundance for the rest of the world, so that everyone may share in good fortune in the years ahead.

- Select a puppy at a shelter and let that puppy remind you what true gratitude is all about as it kisses your face and tucks in contentedly at your feet. Or perhaps a kitten who is purring with pleasure while rubbing its chin against your leg.

- Take a walk—alone or with people—and be thankful for the grandeur of nature. Sniff the lovely smells of autumn.

- Pay for someone else's Thanksgiving dinner—someone who wouldn't be having one without you.

- Take a child for a Thanksgiving drive or stroll, pointing out the blessings in the world around them and how fortunate they are compared with others. Encourage them to do a good deed for the day and demonstrate the power of giving to uplift.

- Meditate for an hour on Thanksgiving Day, and just be in a state of gratitude and peace. That feeds great energy into the world and raises your vibration.

Now here are some things you can do EVERY DAY:

- Start your day or close your day with a list of things, people, and experiences for which you are grateful. Express this as a prayer or blessing.

- Keep a "Gratitude Journal" listing all things for which you are grateful.

Practical Conscious Creation Tip No. 67

Go Green for the Holidays

With our resources becoming more and more precious, you might want to think about ways you can support the planet during this usual time of excess! Make sure to choose wisely for Thanksgiving. Don't over-buy or over-cook, look for ways to be environmentally sensitive in your means of food preparation and disposal, and maybe carpool to dinner with other friends and relatives. For Christmas and Hannukah, is it really necessary to illuminate your house with huge numbers of holiday lights, or can you cut back on the number of bulbs or the hours that they are illuminated? Are there ways to recycle old ribbons, bows, and holiday wrapping, or devise creative methods to decorate brown paper bags? Shop with your own reusable bags instead of going home with plastic or paper bags from your holiday spree. Buy environmentally sustainable products as gifts. Put green gifts on the wish list you give to family and friends. Buy from socially responsible companies. Consider alternatives to a fresh cut Christmas tree. Just be more conscious about your actions and how you can tread more lightly on the planet while you are still enjoying the festive spirit of the holiday season.

- Tell each individual who aids or serves you, not just "thank you" but how grateful you are.

- Write notes of gratitude to people, especially when they don't expect it.

- Always arrive with a gift of gratitude when someone has invited you to their home or to some event. If you cannot afford to buy a gift, make one!

- Bring tokens of gratitude to your co-workers at least once a month.

- Send birthday cards to people you care about with expressions of how grateful you are to have them in your life. This can be by mail or email. You can create reminders with Microsoft Outlook, Facebook or annual calendars on other web-based programs.

- Share your appreciation not just with those to whom you are grateful but with others who know them so that the recipient is aware that you are proud to sing his or her praises.

- Go on a Gratitude Journey—Take a walk, a bike ride, or a cross-country ski trip in the outdoors and just allow your heart to express your gratitude at the beauty and at all things in your life.

- Do a Gratitude Survey—Survey your amazing body and mind, and offer gratitude for each and every part. Don't forget your smile!

- Be thankful for the Universe itself! For without this great force of energy and spirit, you would not exist today as the grateful being you are.

- Believe in the power of gratitude to heal your life, heal the world, and pave your rich and plentiful future.

Happy Thanksgiving! May your gratitude overflow year round and open the door for all the abundance for which to be grateful!

How to Not Let Your Relatives Ring Your Holiday Bell

Are you one of those people who dread the holidays? Last-minute shopping, decorating disasters, difficult people to buy for, demanding kids—and most of all the run-ins with relatives!

If you're anticipating a rerun of previous years where your relatives made you crazy and your holidays were filled with headaches, then you are sure to experience that again this year—because the energy you put into dreading and anticipating will pave the way for more of the same.

However, by Consciously Creating your day—juggling work, shopping, cooking, tree trimming, kids, the management of those pesky relatives—you can have the kind of holiday season you desire effortlessly and without hiccup.

Here are six tips for creating "Relative Harmony" for the Holidays:

1. **Throw out the "love net."** Well before they show up at your door, when you begin planning your holiday, send your "love net"—your high-vibration loving energy—out to your relatives, and keep doing it throughout the holiday season. Feel love toward them even in the most trying times. Know that love is patience and understanding. Plenty of loving energy can head off, diffuse, and transmute negative energy emanating from your relations. Ask for an unending supply of loving energy to pass into you from the Universe and *through* you to your family members.

2. **Visualize.** Take some quiet time each day and visualize just how wonderful your time with your relatives will be. In your mind, see them helping you instead of criticizing, offering support, staying out of the way, picking up after themselves, volunteering instead of demanding, loving the gifts you have picked for them, and finding ways to make your time together joyful and loving. Relish the emotions of these wonderful reunions. Thank the Universe in advance for granting this incredible camaraderie, goodwill, grace and warmth. Then go ahead and visualize the rest of your day going smoothly, too!

3. **Stay in your high-frequency range.** Whatever happens, do not allow your relations to pull you into the low-frequency range of anger, frustration, bitterness, or regret. Stay in your high-frequency states of love, contentment, joy, compassion, and generosity by playing music and tuning out negativity, focusing on those who appreciate what you are offering, and doing something creative that serves your soul. If you are being bombarded by negative energy—excuse yourself and go do something yummy just for you—take in a movie, go for a walk, play with your puppy, give yourself a candlelit bath with soothing essential oils, or go work out.

4. **Redirect them into helping you in a good way.** If you know that they are likely to be under foot, in your way or just over-helpful in the wrong ways, have a list in advance of things you would like them to do to help you in a

Practical Conscious Creation Tip No. 68

Give the Most Precious Gift of Yourself at the Holidays

If you are like many people during the holiday season, then you might be feeling the financial crunch. Your budget for gifts may not be what you had available in the past. This should not be a source of embarrassment or dread; you are being prudent. So I would encourage you to remember that this season is about spiritual reconnection and renewal and the power of love. If you focus on these elements in your gift giving, I am confident that you can use your creativity to devise beautiful gifts of your spirit. These do not need to be costly. They can be letters you write and frame, massages you give, daylong road trips taking someone to a place they've always wanted to go, dinners you cook, books you read to someone whose sight is gone, pictures put in a scrapbook, homemade crafts, or private musical performances. If the spirit of giving is filled with love, it doesn't have to have a dollar value on it. It can be—in the words of Mastercard®—priceless. Enjoy the creative process of becoming a master of spiritual gifting!

"good way." They'll feel valued by being able to help and making you pleased, and you will manifest goodwill on all planes.

5. **Monitor your own verbal expressions with your "love bubble."** Before you say anything that you would regret or that will escalate into warfare, encase yourself in positive, loving energy. Allow your "love bubble" to be a place where you can breathe deeply and transform your negative energy to positive. See cool, calming blue light starting at the top and washing over you down to your toes at the bottom of the bubble. Now step out and say what you need to say in a calm, loving, respectful, constructive, gracious, but firm way. Call upon the "right" words and tone of voice.

6. **Give Santa those "hot buttons" and let him take them back to the North Pole.** You can do all of the above five things, but if you allow your relatives to push those "hot buttons," you'll be back where you started. Make a conscious decision that you are giving those "hot buttons" to Santa—as your gift to yourself. Release those previous memories of pain and angst with your relations and start afresh. If they start down the old path, surprise them and don't engage! Let go of the mind-chatter in your head that gets you crazy and allows them to get your goat. Just decide not to go there. Instead, simply keep telling yourself you deserve joy, peace, goodwill, and kindly relatives at the holidays! And they just might turn out to be what you imagined!

Now go and have a truly happy holiday!

December
Happy Holidays to Earth, Goodwill to Men

As we embark on the holidays each year, it is a happy time for many. We celebrate the themes of peace on Earth, goodwill to men, generosity, kindness, and compassion. For most of us that means giving gifts to our friends and family, the camaraderie of the office Christmas party, sharing holiday dinner with our loved ones, being kind to ornery Aunt Agatha and dropping a dollar into the Salvation Army collection box. That's where our holiday spirit begins and ends because of our busy lives occupied with so much more.

This year you have an opportunity to do something globally meaningful, as well. It only takes a few minutes and requires no money at all! You can send a gift to the planet and the more than 6 trillion people living on it with little hope of a happy holiday. You can create, gift wrap and send your Vision—your intention for a joyful, abundant, environmentally healthy world.

So, let us offer a Vision that can be a chorus for mankind this holiday season. When you sing your next Christmas Carol or hum the Dreidel Song, take a few minutes to say these words in reverence, and place yourself in the emotional space of actually living in this joyful world. Revel in the emotions of being there! Your emotions are like the wrapping that completes the gift to the Universe and gives it the power to manifest. Believe your Vision can make a difference!

Vision for Our Holiday Gift to the Earth

On this day, we give thanks for a world of incredible peace, where only people's voices ring out, not guns, where love abounds everywhere. Just see the kindness and compassion between people wherever we look! It's amazing to view families united in love, forgiving the breaches that have kept them apart. Now look over there and see two former enemies working together in respect and affection. Observe the people of different races and backgrounds agreeing on new ways to make their community a place of prosperity. See leaders speaking truths that unite instead of divide. How fantastic to note financially successful people creating opportunities and helping to uplift the impoverished, and to see the poor prosper and rising into the ranks of the middle class. We are so grateful for the abundant food on everyone's table and the solid well-crafted roofs over their heads. Hear the joyful voices of all the world's children who are reading books and writing beautiful words, skills that they can learn in high-quality schools that are free to attend. Let's celebrate the world's prosperity, where monies are now spent on increasing quality of life for everyone and that growing abundance enables quality time for spirit, play, family and joyful surrender. And as we sit toasty in our homes in the Northern Hemisphere and enjoy the beauty of summer in the Southern Hemisphere, we are so appreciative of all the new forms of sustainable energy that are preserving our environmental balance. We feel blessed by the planet's return to climate balance, the restoration of the animal populations, the healthy slowing of man's birthrate, the protection and preservation of our natural resources, and the creative and sustainable ways that new life has been breathed into our cities and suburbs. Oh what a glorious time to live! Our earth is again breathing clearly and protected by its healthy shell of ozone. It feels safe and empowered with the spirit of goodness and positive energy suffused into it by the all of the world's peoples. We are one with a peaceful and bountiful Universe!

Make this Vision—or one of your own creation—a new part of your annual holiday ritual and know that you are helping to manifest a loving and peaceful planet.

Happy holidays to Earth and goodwill to men!

If Money Were No Object and You Had All of the Time in the World— What Would You Do This Coming Year?

As you begin to embark on an exciting New Year, I'd like to encourage you to breath in the possibilities! Now is the time to release any of the pain and struggle from last year, and unhook yourself from fears related to your financial status. Let go of problems with family and relationships. Forgive yourself for self-judgment and falling short of who you want to be. Release and breathe!

You have a great opportunity to start anew as we usher in the New Year. Let's wipe the slate clean and ask the wonderful question: *What if money were no object, and I had all the time in the world? What would my forthcoming year look like?*

Why should we do this exercise? Because it's the perfect way to start visioning and Consciously Creating your near-term future—and maybe long-term. So what would be in your plans if you could do anything you wanted with your time and energy?

Practical Conscious Creation Tip No. 69

Holiday Rituals

The holidays are a great time to begin new Conscious Creation rituals that will hitch a ride on the wonderful goodwill of the season. Consider starting a tradition featuring a holiday tree where everyone in the family hangs a card containing a wish for something they would like to manifest in the New Year! Or place in a stocking a vision for someone else so that you are "giving" a wish of Conscious Creation for someone who might be ill or who needs "light" in their life. Do a "pay-it-forward" holiday practice where each person performs a good deed for another. Establish a Conscious Creation intention with every Hannukah candle that is lit—one for you and the next one for someone you know! Allow this festive time to be an incubator for Conscious Creation visions and wishes that can manifest in the next year.

Here's what I would do if my bank account overflowed with cash, my financial future was set, and all of my debts and bills were paid: I would be out leading people in major visioning events to set the course for the world's future. I would continue to travel all over the world teaching *Practical Conscious Creation* in seminars, speeches, and lectures. As I travel, I would be taking stunning photos for my Lapin Gallery photo website, and sharing this wonderful experience with my incredible lover and friend who has come into my life. I'd be enjoying the fantastic success of my latest three books, while at the same time finding plenty of opportunity to rest and relax in nature, read, exercise, do yoga, and live in the moment. Furthermore, I would be giving my time, leadership skills, and money to worthy causes, organizations, and individuals—helping people of little means and opportunity live more empowered, directed, abundant, and prosperous lives.

Now, what would your life look like?

- Where would you live?
- Whom would you be with?
- How would you spend your time—both leisure time and constructive time?
- Would you still work? If so, what would you be doing?
- What causes would you champion? How would that manifest?
- What would you want to learn or teach?
- What creative endeavor or outlet would you pursue?
- What recreational experience would you like to have?
- Where would you travel? What would you see or do?
- What do you want more of in your life?
- What would your relationship be like?
- What would be different about your relationship with your family?
- What kinds of friends would you like to have?
- How would you manifest greater health and vitality?
- What spiritual or meditative practices would you adopt or do more often?
- What would you do to increase your personal frequency, be more positive, and release negative vibrations such as fear?

Practical Conscious Creation Tip No. 70

Reboot!

Okay, so the weather may be dismal, you're struggling a bit financially, and you're buying into the lack mystique that's permeating the nation. You feel stagnated and you're giving in to depression. So take a break from the doom and gloom! It's not any fun anyway.

Here's what I do: a reboot! I take the week between Christmas and New Years and reset my mental attitude. Last year, I read 13 powerful spiritual books, then sat down to meditate and connect to the Universe. Filled with that inspiration, I decided everything was going to be fun and abundant, and I settled into that vibration. Most importantly, I consciously called forth the vibration of love—coming into me and through me—so that I could then pass it along to others. I dwelled in those emotions and visualizations for a couple of hours each day, feeling them welling up inside me.

And guess what? Very shortly afterward, I had a flood of new business calls, lots of great opportunities, and a good bit more fun and joy. So if you're feeling down, it's time for a reboot! You can do it anytime!

I suggest that you take some time before New Year's Eve and consider these questions, because they can create a blueprint for next year. Don't leave it to chance. Be specific.

Now, keep in mind that not everything is likely to come to pass immediately unless you were to perhaps win the lottery. But you are submitting your "wish list" to the cosmic Santa and allowing him to get the elves working on it. Some elements may begin to manifest or start evolving in the direction you desire. *However, if you don't do this* you are at the whim of whatever unconscious frequencies you are transmitting—and who knows what will turn up in your life this next year?!

Take this time and put these important thoughts on paper, then look back one year from now to see how many of them have come to fruition! Hone your manifesting skills. Take charge of your future. Live the life of your dreams . . . starting NOW!

Chapter 14

Creating Your Own Practical Conscious Creation Practices

By now, you should be getting your bearings when it comes to incorporating Conscious Creation into your daily life. These mini-lessons are templates on ways that you can adapt positive, optimistic, unlimited, empowering, and forward thinking into your existence. Conscious Creation should be an underlying influence in all of your actions, decisions, routines, practices, and challenges.

How can you continue to adapt and employ these concepts to continue expansive growth in your life?

- Use your inner guidance system to know when you need to make a course correction. Then see how you can recharge the experience with upbeat, positive, and visually rich imaging.

- Activate your imagination to develop creative ways to keep you thinking abundantly and expansively (see A Dialogue Between You and Your Money).

- Look at the areas in your life where you are less successful. Consider what fun or empowering Conscious Creation practices can be applied to jumpstart greater success. Think of yourself as one of those CEOs brought in to help a company make a turnaround.

- When faced with a challenge, what advice would you give yourself if you were a Conscious Creation coach?

- When embracing a need to grow, evolve, or change, list specific actions you can take that will help you move forward in an empowering Conscious Creation manner.

- When fear or resistance are holding you back, reach for the courage that you have cultivated through this process and believe in the techniques you learned to carry you to a positive outcome.

Rewire your mind to think like a Conscious Creator, and it will infuse everything you do with the power to change your life in incredible and amazing ways. Your rewards for adapting Practical Conscious Creation as a way of life are personal freedom, unbounded success, unconditional love, and joyful living.

May You Consciously Create All You Desire!

My Gifts to You…

Thank you for reading *Practical Conscious Creation!* I hope that this is only the beginning of new horizons and an exciting, fulfilling future for you as you begin implementing the guidance in this book. In order to continue your mastery in manifesting, I would like to make a gift to you of other beneficial tools.

- The Practical Conscious Creation Vault, a growing compendium of articles that offers new approaches and techniques for Consciously Creating your life. Keep your *Practical Conscious Creation* recipe book fresh with new recipes! *www.PracticalConsciousCreation.com/vault*

- *The Conscious Creation Chronicle Newsletter*, twice a month newsletters with brand new articles just like the ones you read in this book, plus much more! *www.JackieLapin.com*

- *The Manifest Messenger*, daily tips sent to you by email… with new inspirations for Conscious Creation every day! We've selected the very best manifesting advice from the most gifted wisdom teachers today and yesterday. *www.JackieLapin.com*

- My Conscious Creation Blog. *www.JackieLapin.com/blog*

- Special programs and personal interaction. When you register at *www.JackieLapin.com*, you'll be among the first to know of special Practical Conscious Creation programs we offer, coaching calls, discounts on learning tools, and my personal appearances near you—where you can come and introduce yourself!

- A $5 gift coupon toward the purchase of *The Art of Conscious Creation, How You Can Transform the World*. Use this code when purchasing the book exclusively at *www.JackieLapin.com*: PCCGIFT. *The Art of Conscious Creation* is a wonderful companion book to *Practical Conscious Creation*. Here what's been said about it:

    o Dr. Joe Vitale, star of *The Secret* and author of *The Attractor Factor*: "An astonishing book! ... the first paint-by-the-numbers approach to creating a personal and planetary life that is abundant and happy for all."

    o Mark Victor Hansen, co-creator of *Chicken Soup for the Soul*: "If you're ready to create your personal world into a veritable 'Garden of Eden,' read, drink in deeply these profound insights and together let's positively change the world."

    o And here's what people just like you have said: "life-changing," "empowering," "transforming," "inspiring," "eye-opening," "amazing," "enlightening," "breakthrough," "brilliant," and "exactly what I needed."

- Come join me on *LifeWisdomNetwork.com*, the Virtual Village that is THE marketplace, directory and information resource for the fast-growing Consciousness and Transformational world, connecting Conscious people with Conscious resources. A place where you will find Conscious Authors & Experts, Performers, Retailers, Businesses, Media, Practitioners, Products, Organizations, Events and more…everything you need to lead a Practical Conscious Creation lifestyle! *www.LifeWisdomNetwork.com*

From my heart to yours…in light and love, —Jackie Lapin

FINDHORN PRESS

Life-Changing Books

Consult our catalogue online (with secure order facility) on
www.findhornpress.com